Dedication

Moaz Safi Yousef al-Kasasbeh
May 29, 1988 – January 3, 2015

Also by Yatir Nitzany

Conversational Spanish Quick and Easy

Conversational French Quick and Easy

Conversational Italian Quick and Easy

Conversational Portuguese Quick and Easy

Conversational German Quick and Easy

Conversational Russian Quick and Easy

Conversational Hebrew Quick and Easy

Conversational Yiddish Quick and Easy

Conversational Polish Quick and Easy

Conversational Arabic Quick and Easy
Lebanese Dialect

Conversational Arabic Quick and Easy
Palestinian Arabic

Conversational Arabic Quick and Easy
Jordanian Dialect

Conversational Arabic Quick and Easy
Emirati Dialect

Conversational
Arabic
Quick and Easy

NORTH AFRICAN DIALECTS

YATIR NITZANY

Copyright © 2017
Yatir Nitzany
All rights reserved.
ISBN-13: 978-1-951244-34-7

Printed in the United States of America

Foreword

About Myself

For many years I struggled to learn Spanish, and I still knew no more than about twenty words. Consequently, I was extremely frustrated. One day I stumbled upon this method as I was playing around with word combinations. Suddenly, I came to the realization that every language has a certain core group of words that are most commonly used and, simply by learning them, one could gain the ability to engage in quick and easy conversational Spanish.

I discovered which words those were, and I narrowed them down to three hundred and fifty that, once memorized, one could connect and create one's own sentences. The variations were and are *infinite*! By using this incredibly simple technique, I could converse at a proficient level and speak Spanish. Within a week, I astonished my Spanish-speaking friends with my newfound ability. The next semester I registered at my university for a Spanish language course, and I applied the same principles I had learned in that class (grammar, additional vocabulary, future and past tense, etc.) to those three hundred and fifty words I already had memorized, and immediately I felt as if I had grown wings and learned how to fly.

At the end of the semester, we took a class trip to San José, Costa Rica. I was like a fish in water, while the rest of my classmates were floundering and still struggling to converse. Throughout the following months, I again applied the same principle to other languages—French, Portuguese, Italian, and Arabic, all of which I now speak proficiently, thanks to this very simple technique.

This method is by far the fastest way to master quick and easy conversational language skills. There is no other technique that compares to my concept. It is effective, it worked for me, and it will work for you. Be consistent with my program, and you too will succeed the way I and many, many others have.

Contents

Introduction to the Program 8
Memorization Made Easy 11
Egyptian Arabic. 12
Libyan Arabic. 45
Moroccan Arabic. 77
Tunisian Arabic. 109
Algerian Arabic. 141
Conclusion 171

INTRODUCTION TO THE PROGRAM

People often dream about learning a foreign language, but usually they never do it. Some feel that they just won't be able to do it while others believe that they don't have the time. Whatever your reason is, it's time to set that aside. With my new method, you will have enough time, and you will not fail. You will actually learn how to speak the fundamentals of the language—fluently in as little as a few days. Of course, you won't speak perfect North African dialects at first, but you will certainly gain significant proficiency. For example, if you travel to Egypt, Libya, Morocco, Tunisia, or Algeria you will almost effortlessly be able engage in basic conversational communication with the locals in the present tense and you will no longer be intimidated by culture shock. It's time to relax. Learning a language is a valuable skill that connects people of multiple cultures around the world—and you now have the tools to join them.

How does my method work? I have taken twenty-seven of the most commonly used languages in the world and distilled from them the three hundred and fifty most frequently used words in any language. This process took three years of observation and research, and during that time, I determined which words I felt were most important for this method of basic conversational communication. In that time, I chose these words in such a way that they were structurally interrelated and that, when combined, form sentences. Thus, once you succeed in memorizing these words, you will be able to combine these words and form your own sentences. The words are spread over twenty pages. The words will also combine easily in sentences, for example, enabling you to ask

Introduction to the Program

simple questions, make basic statements, and obtain a rudimentary understanding of others' communications. In fact, there are just nine basic words that will effectively build bridges, enabling you to speak in an understandable manner (please see Building Bridges). I have also created Memorization Made Easy techniques for this program in order to help with the memorization of the vocabulary. Please also see Reading and Pronunciation of Arabic accents in order to gain proficiency in the reading and pronunciation of the Arabic language prior to starting this program

My book is mainly intended for basic present tense vocal communication, meaning anyone can easily use it to "get by" linguistically while visiting a foreign country without learning the entire language. With practice, you will be 100 percent understandable to native speakers, which is your aim. One disclaimer: this is *not* a grammar book, though it does address minute and essential grammar rules. Therefore, understanding complex sentences with obscure words in Arabic is beyond the scope of this book.

People who have tried this method have been successful, and by the time you finish this book, you will understand and be understood in basic conversational Arabic. This is the best basis to learn not only the Arabic language but any language. This is an entirely revolutionary, no-fail concept, and your ability to combine the pieces of the "language puzzle" together will come with great ease, especially if you use this program prior to beginning an Arabic class.

This is the best program that was ever designed to teach the reader how to become conversational. Other conversational programs will only teach you phrases. But this is the only program that will teach you how to create your own sentences for the purpose of becoming conversational.

MEMORIZATION MADE EASY

There is no doubt the three hundred and fifty words in my program are the required essentials in order to engage in quick and easy basic conversation in any foreign language. However, some people may experience difficulty in the memorization. For this reason, I created Memorization Made Easy. This memorization technique will make this program so simple and fun that it's unbelievable! I have spread the words over the following twenty pages. Each page contains a vocabulary table of ten to fifteen words. Below every vocabulary box, sentences are composed from the words on the page that you have just studied. This aids greatly in memorization. Once you succeed in memorizing the first page, then proceed to the second page. Upon completion of the second page, go back to the first and review. Then proceed to the third page. After memorizing the third, go back to the first and second and repeat. And so on. As you continue, begin to combine words and create your own sentences in your head. Every time you proceed to the following page, you will notice words from the previous pages will be present in those simple sentences as well, because repetition is one of the most crucial aspects in learning any foreign language. Upon completion of your twenty pages, *congratulations*, you have absorbed the required words and gained a basic, quick-and-easy proficiency and you should now be able to create your own sentences and say anything you wish in the North African Arabic dialects. This is a crash course in conversational Arabic, and it works!

Conversational Arabic Quick and Easy

EGYPTIAN ARABIC

YATIR NITZANY

EGYPTIAN ARABIC

Although the official language of Egypt is Modern Standard Arabic, its people speak Egyptian Arabic. Written in the Arabic alphabet, the language is spoken by over 77 million people throughout the world, though mostly concentrated in Egypt. Unlike Modern Standard Arabic, most people speak Egyptian Arabic at social occasions, though it is also used in some common examples like newspapers and street signs. Egyptian Arabic originated in the areas around Alexandria and Cairo, which have always led the country economically. Historically, the ancient Muslim expeditions to Egypt resulted in an increase in the Arabic language, but shifted back to Egyptian when Muslim troops, speaking an Egyptian dialect, inhabited the area.

Spoken in: Egypt

ARABIC PRONUNCIATIONS

PLEASE MASTER THE FOLLOWING PAGE IN ARABIC PRONUNCIATIONS PRIOR TO STARTING THE PROGRAM

Kha. For Middle Eastern languages including Arabic, Hebrew, Farsi, Pashto, Urdu, Hindi, etc., and also German, to properly pronounce the kh or ch is essential, for example, *Khaled* (a Muslim name) or *Chanukah* (a Jewish holiday) or *Nacht* ("night" in German). The best way to describe kh or ch is to say "ka" or "ha" while at the same time putting your tongue at the back of your throat and blowing air. It's pronounced similarly to the sound that you make when clearing your throat. Please remember this whenever you come across any word containing a *kh* in this program.

Ghayin. The Arabic *gh* is equivalent to the "g" in English, but its pronunciation more closely resembles the French "r," rather than "g." Pronounce it at the back of your throat. The sound is equivalent to what you would make when gargling water. *Gha* is pronounced more as "rha," rather than as "ga." *Ghada* is pronounced as "rhada." In this program, the symbol for *ghayin* is *gh*, so keep your eyes peeled.

Aayin is pronounced as a'a, pronounced deep at the back of your throat. Rather similar to the sound one would make when gagging. In the program, the symbol for *aayin* is *a'a, u'u, o'o*, or *i'i*.

Ha is pronounced as *"ha."* Pronunciation takes place deep at the back of your throat, and for correct pronunciation, one must constrict the back of the throat and exhale air while simultaneously saying "ha." In the program, this strong h (*"ha"*) is emphasized whenever *ha, ah, hi, he,* or *hu* is encountered.

J and *G*. In Egyptian Arabic, *j* doesn't exist; it's pronounced as *"g."* In Classical Arabic, "I need" is *ana mihtaj*. However, in Egyptian colloquial dialect, "I need" is pronounced as *ana mihtag*.

NOTE TO THE READER

The purpose of this book is merely to enable you to communicate in Egyptian Arabic. In the program itself (pages 17-39) you may notice that the composition of some of those sentences might sound rather clumsy. This is intentional. These sentences were formulated in a specific way to serve two purposes: to facilitate the easy memorization of the vocabulary and to teach you how to combine the words in order to form your own sentences for quick and easy communication, rather than making complete literal sense in the English language. So keep in mind that this is not a phrase book!

As the title suggests, the sole purpose of this program is for conversational use only. It is based on the mirror translation technique. These sentences, as well as the translations are not incorrect, just a little clumsy. Latin languages, Semitic languages, and Anglo-Germanic languages, as well as a few others, are compatible with the mirror translation technique.

Many users say that this method surpasses any other known language learning technique that is currently out there on the market. Just stick with the program and you will achieve wonders!

Note to the Reader

Again, I wish to stress this program is by no means, shape, or form a phrase book! The sole purpose of this book is to give you a fundamental platform to enable you to connect certain words to become conversational. Please also read the "Introduction" and the "About Me" section prior to commencing the program.

In order to succeed with my method, please start on the very first page of the program and fully master one page at a time prior to proceeding to the next. Otherwise, you will overwhelm yourself and fail. Please do not skip pages, nor start from the middle of the book.

It is a myth that certain people are born with the talent to learn a language, and this book disproves that myth. With this method, anyone can learn a foreign language as long as he or she follows these explicit directions:

* Memorize the vocabulary on each page

* Follow that memorization by using a notecard to cover the words you have just memorized and test yourself.

* Then read the sentences following that are created from the vocabulary bank that you just mastered.

* Once fully memorized, give yourself the green light to proceed to the next page.

Again, if you proceed to the following page without mastering the previous, you are guaranteed to gain nothing from this book. If you follow the prescribed steps, you will realize just how effective and simplistic this method is.

THE PROGRAM

Let's Begin! "Vocabulary"
(memorize the vocabulary)

I | I am	Ana
With you	Ma'ak / ma'aki
With him / with her	Ma'aah- ma'aaha
With us	Ma'ana
For you	(Masc) Leek / (Fem) Leeky
Without him	Min ghairu
Without them	Min ghairhum
Always	Dayman
Was	Kan
This, This is	Da
Is, it's, it is	Huwwa
Sometimes	Sa'at *or* Ahyanan
Maybe	Yimkin
Are you? / is it?	(M)Hal inta?(F)hal inti?/hal huwwa
Better	Ahsan
You, you are	(M)Inta / (F)inti
He / She	Huwwa/Hiyya
From	Min

Sentences from the vocabulary (now you can speak the sentences and connect the words)

I am with you
Ana ma'aak

This is for you
(M)Da ashanak/(F)Da ashanik

I am from Egypt
Ana min Masr

Are you from Iraq?
Inta min Il-Iraq?

Sometimes you are with us at the mall
Sa'at/ahyanan bitkun inta ma'ana fil mall

I am always with her
Ana dayman ma'aaha

Are you without them today?
Inta mish ma'ahum innaharda?

Sometimes I am with him
Ahyanan ana bakun ma'aah

*In Arabic, there are gender rules. Saying "for you" to a male is *leek*, but if you are talking to a female then it's *leeky*. In spoken Arabic, which has no rules, they do say, *Il kitab da lik*, but they also say, *Ilkitab da ashanak*, or *Ilkitab da bita'ak*.

*In spoken Arabic, words like *hal* / "are" are usually dropped, and we only say *Hiyya aklat? Huwwa Nayim?*, etc., which, if written in Classical Arabic, would have been *Hal akalat hiya?* or *Hal huwa Na'im?*

I was	Ana Kunt
To be	(M)Ykun/(F)Tikun
The	Il, al
Same / like *(as in similar)*	Zay/mitl/nafs
Good	Kwayyis
Here	Hina
Very	Giddan/Awi
And	Wi
Between	Bain
Now	Dilwa'ti
Later / After / afterwards	Ba'din/Ba'd kidah
If	Lau
Yes	Aywah
To	Li
Tomorrow	Bukrah
Person	Insan/bani adam/shakhs
Also / too / as well	Kaman/bardu

If it was between now and later
Lau kan da bain dilwa'ti wi ba'dain
It's better tomorrow
Yufaddal bukrah
This is good as well
Da bardu kwayyis
To be the same person
Yikun nafs ilshakhs
Yes, you are very good
Aywah, inta kwayyis awi
I was here with them
Ana kunt hina ma'ahum
You and I
Inta wa ana
The same day
Nafs innahar

*In the Arabic language, adjectives follow the noun. For example, "the same day" is *nafs innahar*, "small house" is *beit zrir*, "tall person" is *shakhs tawil*, and "short person" is *shakhs aseer*.

*In this program, the article "the" *(il, al)* will sometimes become a prefix at the beginning of the noun. For nouns beginning with *d, n, r, s, sh, t, th,* and *z*, the *l* is omitted and replaced with the initial consonant of the following noun. "The people" /*al-shakhs* is *ishakhs*. The Nile *il-nil* is *inil*. It is dropped when spoken; however, when written, it's usually *il-shaks* or *il-nil*.

*In Egpytian Arabic the definition of *nafs* is *same*, however *same* as in *like* (preposition form) is *zay/mitl*.

The Program

Me	Ana, ni, li
Ok	Tayyib
Even if	Hatta law
No	La/ma
Worse	Aswa'a
Where	Fain
Everything	Kul hagah
Somewhere	Fi makanin ma
What	Aih?
Almost	Kunti khalas/Arrabt
There	Hinak
I go	Ana rayih

Afterwards is worse
Ba'dain haykun aswa'a
Even if I go now
Hatta lau ruht dilwa'ti
Where is everything?
Fain kul hagah?
Maybe somewhere
Yimkin fi makanin ma
What? I am almost there
Aih? Ana Arrabt akun hnak
Where are you?
Inta fain?

Fi makan literally means "in a place."
*In Arabic the pronoun "me" has several definitions. In relation to verbs, it's *ni, li*. *Li* refers to any verb that relates to action of doing something to someone or for someone. For example, "tell me," "tell (to) me" / *ul li*. Ni just means "me": "love me" / *hibbini*. "On me" is *alayya*, "in me" is *fiyya / biyya*, and "to me" is *liyya*. "With me" is ma'ayah, "in front of me" is *ussadi*, and "from me" is *minni*. The same rule applies for "him" and "her"; both become suffixes: *hu* and *ha*.
- "love her" / *hebbaha*
- "love him" / *hibbih*
- "love them" and "love us" / *hibbihum* and *hibbina*
Any verb that relates to doing something to someone, for someone put *l*.
Tell me *Ul'li*, tell him *Ul'luh*, tell her *Ul'laha*, tell them *Ul'luhum*, tell us *Ul'lina*.
Adding "you" as a suffix in Arabic is *ak* or *lak*. Female *ik* or *lik*.
"Love you" / *Bahibbak, Bahibbik*, "tell you" / *A'ullak* (f.) *A'ullik*.
*In Egyptian Arabic, there are a few ways of saying "no," depending on where it falls in the sentence. You can say, *Ma fish faydah*, but if asked something like, "Are you going?" you would answer, "*Laa*."

House	Bait
In, at, at the	Fi/ala
Car	Arabeyah
Already	Khalas
Good morning	Sabah ilkhair
How are you?	Izzayak?
Where are you from?	(M)Inta min fain?(F)Inti min fain?
Today	Innaharda
Hello	Ahlan
What is your name?	Ismak Aih?/ Ismik Aih
How old are you?	Andak kam sana
Son	Ibn
Daughter	Bint
To have	(M)Anduh/(F)andaha
Doesn't or isn't	Ma or mish
Hard	Sa'b
Still	Lissah/bardu

She doesn't have a car, so maybe she is still at the house?
Hiyya ma andahash arabeyah, yimkin hiyya lissah fil bait
I am in the car already with your son and daughter
Ana khalas fil arabeyah ma' ibnak wi bintak
Good morning, how are you today?
Sabah al-khair, izzayak innaharda?
Hello, what is your name?
Ahlan, inta ismak aih?
How old are you?
Andak kam sana?
This is very hard, but it's not impossible
Da sa'b awi, bas mish mustahil
Where are you from?
Inta min fain?

*In Egyptian Arabic, possessive pronouns become suffixes to the noun. For example, in the translation for "your," *ak* is the masculine form, and *ik* is the feminine form.
-"your book" / *kitabak* (m.), *kitabik* (f.)
- "your house" / *baitak* (m.), *baitik* (f.)
*In the Arabic language, as well as in other Semitic languages, the article "a" doesn't exist. "She doesn't have a car" / *hiyya ma indahash arabeyah*.
*The definition of *khalas* can also be "done" or "finished."

The Program

Thank you	Mutshakkir
For	Ala
Anything	Kol hagah/ayyi hagah
That, That is	Dah
Time	Wa't
But	Lakin
No/ Not	La'/abadan
I am not	Ana mish
Away	Bi'id
Late	Mit'akkhar
Similar, like	Zay/Mitl
Another/ Other	Tani
Side	Ganb, Taraf
Until	Lahad
Yesterday	Imbarih
Without us	Min ghairna
Since	Min sa'at
Day	Nahar/Yum
Before	Abl

Thanks for anything
Mutshakkir ala ayyi hagah
It's already time
Ilwa'ti khalas geh (*gah* means *arrive/come*)
I am not here, I am outside
Ana mish hina, ana barrah
That is a similar house
Ilbait da zayyuh
I am from the other side
Ana min innahyah il tanyah
But I was here until late yesterday
Lakin ana kont hina mit'akkhar imbarih
I am not at the other house
Ana mish fil bait iltani

*In Egyptian Arabic, there are three definitions for time:
* "time" / *wa't* refers to "era", "moment period," "duration of time."
* "time(s)" / *marra(t)* refers to "occasion" or "frequency."
* "time" / *sa'ah* references "hour," "what time is it?"
Ayyi or *ayyu* depending on where it falls in the sentence. This is the *ay* in Classical Arabic, meaning "any." We stress the y, because this is how it is pronounced in Egyptian.

Conversational Arabic Quick and Easy

I say / I am saying	Ana Ba'ul
What time is it?	Issa'ah kam?
I want	Ana Awiz
Without you	Min ghairak
Everywhere /wherever	Fi kol makan/ Fi ay makan
I am going	(M) Ana rayih /(F) Ana rayhah
With	Ma'
My	Liyya
Cousin	(M) Ibni amm (or) Ibni khal [uncle from mother's side), (P) Awlad amm /Awlad Khal (F)bint amm/ bint khal, (P)banat amm, banat khal
I need	Ana mihtag, Ana bihagah
Right now	Dilwa'itti
Night	Lail
To see	Ashuf
Light	Nur
Outside	Barrah
Without	Min ghair
Happy	Mabsut/Farhan
I see / I am seeing	Ana shayif

I am saying no / I say no
Ana ba'ul la'a/ ba'ul la'a
I want to see this today
Ana awiz ashuf dah innaharda
I am with you everywhere
Ana ma'aka fi kol makan
I am happy without my cousins here
Ana mabsut min ghair awlad ammi hina
I need to be there at night
Ana lazim akun hinak bil-lail
I see light outside
Ana shayif nur barrah
What time is it right now?
Issa'ah kam dilwa'ti

*"My" / li is also a possessive pronoun.
Li means "my" but also becomes a suffix to a noun, for example:
* "cousin" / awlad il'am, my cousin / ibn ammi or ibn khali [maternal uncle's son]
* "cup" / kubbayah, "my cup" / kubbayti
For second and third person masculine noun; ibn ("son"), male (ak, akum) and female (ik, ikum). For example: "your son" / ibnak (m.), ibnik (f.), "your (plural) son" / ibnukum (m.) ibnukum (f.) [In Egyptian, unlike Classical Arabic, plural female is not different from plural male.], "his son" / ibnu, "her son" / ibnaha, "our son" / ibnina, "their son / ibnuhum (m.&f.)
For second and third person, we use a feminine noun: "car" / arabeyah.
* "your car, arabiyyitak, "your (plural) car" / arabiyyitkum, "his car" / arabiyyittu, "her car" / arabiyyit-ha

Place	Makan
Easy	Sahl
To find	Yila'i
To look for/to search	Adawwar
Near / Close	Urayyib
To wait	Astanna
To sell	Abi'i
To use	Asta'mil
To know	A'raf
To decide	Aqarar
Between	Bain
Next to	Ganb
To	Li

This place it's easy to find
Ilmakan dah sahl yit-la'a
I want to look for this next to the car
Ana awiz adawwar ala dah ganb il-arabeyah
I am saying to wait until tomorrow
Ana ba'ul nistana lehad bukrah
This table is easy to sell
Il-tarabaizah di sahl titba'a
I want to use this
Ana awiz asta'mil dah
I need to know where is the house
Ana mihtag a'raf makan il-bait
I want to decide between both places
Ana awiz aqarar bain il makanain

*Please pay close attention to the conjugation of verbs, whether they are in first person, second, or third. Unlike Anglo-Germanic languages, Latin languages, or even Classical Arabic, in which the first verb is conjugated and the following is always infinitive, in colloquial Arabic, it is quite different. In spoken Arabic, for example, for the first-person tense, the first verb is conjugated into first person and the following verb as well. For example, "I need to know where is the house," in Classical Arabic, it is *Innani bihajah* ("I need") *ila ma'rifat* ("to know" ["to know" is infinitive]) *makan al-manzil*. In Egyptian Arabic, it is *Ana mihtag* ("I need") a'raf (the verb "to know" is conjugated into first person as well) *makan il-bait*. The same rules apply to second as well as third person. Keep in mind: The Egyptian dialect of the Arabic language is considered a colloquial, rather than an official language.
Makan il-bait literally means the "location/place of the house."

Because	Ashan
To buy	Ashtiri
Life	Ilhayah, ilumr
Them, They	Humma
Bottle	Izazah
Book	Kitab
Mine	Bita'i
To understand	Afham
Problem / Problems	Mushkilah/mashakil
I do / I am doing	A'mal/ ana ba'mal
Of	Min
To look	Bytul
Myself	Nafsi
Enough	Kifayah
Food / water	Akl/Mayyah
Each/ every/ all /entire	Kol,kolokom,gamee'hom
Hotel	Fundu'

I like this hotel because I want to look at the beach
Ana agibni il Fundu' dah ashan bytul ala ilshat
I want to buy a bottle of water
Ana awiz ashtiri izazit mayyah
I do this every day
Ana ba'mil kidah kol yaum
Both of them have enough food
Humma litnain andhom akl kifayah
That is the book, and that book is mine
Huwwa dah il-kitab, wil kitab dah bita'i
I need to understand the problem
Ana mihtag afham il mushkilah
I see the view of the city from the hotel
Ana shayif manzar il madina min il Fundu'
I do my homework today
Ana ha'amal ilwagib il manzili innahardah
My entire life/ all my life
Tul Umri/ tul hayati

Tul literally means "the length of."
*"Bottle of water" / *zujajat ma'a* (The use of "of" isn't always required in Arabic.)
Kidah means "like this" or "this way."

The Program

I like	Ana bahib, agebny
There is / There are	Fi
Family / Parents	Ahl/ Il-walidain
Why	Laih
To say	Yi'ul
Something	Hagah
To go	Yiruh
Ready	Gahiz
Soon	Urayyib
To work	A'mil/Asawwi
Who	Min
Busy	Mashgul
That (conjunction)	Innuh
I Must	Ana lazim / yagib alayya
Important	Muhimmah

I like to be at my house with my parents
Ana bahib akun fi baiti ma'a mamti wa babayah
I want to know why I need to say something important
Ana awiz a'raf laih lazim a'ul hagah muhimmah
I am there with her
Ana hinak ma'aha
I am busy, but I need to be ready soon
Ana mashghul, lakin mihtag agahz bisur'ah
I like to go to work
Ana bahib aruh isshughl
Who is there?
Min hinak?
I want to know if they are here, because I want to go outside
Awiz a'raf iza kanu hina, ashan awiz akhrug barrah
There are seven dolls
Mawgud sab'a li'ab
I need to know that that is a good idea
Ana mihtag a'raf inni di fikrah kwayyisah

*In the last sentence, we use "that" as a conjunction (*innu / inni*) and as a demonstrative pronoun (*da / di*).
Bisur'ah literally means "quickly."
Mawgud literally means "exist," but it also means "there is" or "there are" or "present."
*In Egyptian Arabic, "to go" is *ruh*, however, "to go out" is *akhrug*.

How much /How many	Bikam? Kam wahid?
To bring	Yigib
With me	Ma'aya
Instead	Badal/badal min
Only	Bas / Mugarrad
When	Lamma
I can / Can I?	Ana a'adar/ ba'dar?
Or	Walla/aw
Were	Kan
Without me	Min ghairi
Fast	Sari'i
Slow	Bati'i
Cold	Sa'e'
Inside	Guwwa
To eat	Akol
Hot	Sukhn
To Drive	Yesoo'

How much money do I need to bring with me?
Ana mihtag agib addi aih felus ma'ayah?
Instead of this cake, I want that cake
Badal el gateaux da, ana awez el gateaux da
Only when you can
Bas lamma ti'dar
They were without me yesterday
Kanu min ghairi imbarih
Do I need to drive the car fast or slow?
Ana mihtag asu'u il arabeyah bisur'ah aw bibut'u?
It is cold inside the library
Il gaw sa'e' guwwa il maktaba
Yes, I like to eat this hot for my lunch
Aywah, ana biyi'gibni akol il ghada sukhn bil shakli dah
I can work today
Ana a'dar ashtaghal innaharda

*"Were" is *kan*, but for "they were," add the suffix to the pronoun *kanu*. "We were" is *kunna*.
*In Egyptian Arabic, *addi aih fulus* literally translated means "how much money." In Egyptian Arabic, money can be either *imlah* or *fulus*.
*In Egyptian Arabic, *il gaw* means "the climate, weather, temperature, etc."
*Bil shakli *dah* literally means "this way." However, when we say, *sukhn bil shakli dah*, we are saying "this hot."

The Program

To answer	Il-igabah/ yigawib
To fly	Tayaran/yitir
Time / Times	Marrah/marrat
To travel	Asafer, yesafer
To learn	Yit'allam
How	Izzay
To swim	Yisbah
To practice	Yitdarrab
To play	Yil'ab
To leave (something)	Yissib
Many /much /a lot	Kitir/Adad kibir
I go to	Ana rayih ala
First	Awwal
Time / Times	Wa't, sa'ah/ Aw'at/sa'at
Around	Hawali

I want to answer many questions
Ana awiz agawib ala as'ilah kitirah
I must travel to Dubai today
Ana mihtag [or Lazim] asafir ala Dubai innahardah
I need to learn how to swim at the pool
Ana lazim at'allam issibaha fe birkit il mayyah
I want to learn to play better tennis
Ana awiz at'allam li'b il tennis kuwayyis
I want to leave this here for you when I go to travel the world
Ana awiz asib dah hina ashanak, lamma asafer hawla il-alam
Since the first time
Min awwil marrah
The children are yours
Dul awladak

*In Egyptian Arabic, "to leave (something)" is *asib*. "To leave (a place)" is *asib (il makan)*.
*In Egyptian Arabic, there are three definitions for time:
* "time" / *wa't* refers to "era", "moment period," "duration of time."
* "time(s)" / *marra(t)* refers to "occasion" or "frequency."
* "time" / *sa'ah* references "hour," "what time is it?"
Dul literally means "those" but again, when we want to say 'the children are yours' in Egyptian, we do say "*dul awladak*" meaning the children in question, or the children referred to.
*With the knowledge you've gained so far, now try to create your own sentences!

Conversational Arabic Quick and Easy

Nobody / Anyone	Wala hadd/ayyi hadd
Against	Dud/mish ma'a
Us	Ihna
To visit	Yizur
Mom / Mother	Mama/ummi
To give	Yo'ti
Which	Ayyi
To meet	Yaltaqi
Someone	Hadd
Just	Mugarrad/bas
To walk	Il mashi'
Week	Usbu'u / gum'ah
Towards	Bittigah
Than	Min
Nothing	Wala hagah

Something is better than nothing
Hagah afdal min wala hagah
I am against her
Ana dedaha / Ana mesh ma'aha (*mesh ma'ah* means *without her*)
We go to visit my family each week
Ihna binzur ahli kulli usbu'u
I need to give you something
Ana mihtag addik hagah
Do you want to go meet someone?
Awiz tiruh ti'abil hadd?
I was here on Wednesdays as well
Ana Kaman kunti hina ayyam il-arba'a
Do you do this everyday?
Inta bti'mal kidah kulli yum?
You need to walk, but not towards the house
Inta lazim titmasha, bas mish bi ittigah il-bait

*In Egyptian Arabic, when using the pronoun "you" as a direct and indirect object pronoun (the person who is actually affected by the action being carried out) in relation to a verb, the pronoun, "you," becomes a suffix to that verb. That suffix becomes *ak* (masc.), *ik* (fem.)
* "to give" / *yiddi*: "to give you" / *yiddik*
* "to tell" / *yi'ul*: "to tell you" / *yi'ullak* (m.), *yi'ullik* (f.)
* "see you" / *ashufak*: "to see you" (plural), *ashufkum* (m.), *ashufkum* (f.)
[In Egyptian, they address males and females the same.]
For third person male, add u (hum, plural), and for female, add ha (hum, plural).
* "tell him" / *a'ullu*
* "tell her" / *a'ullaha*
* "see them / *ashufhum* (m.), *ashufhum* (f.)
* "see us" / *shuf*na
*The definition of *I'mal kidah* is "do this" or "do it like this."

The Program

I have	Ana andi
Don't	Mesh
Friend	Sahib/ Sahbiti [F], Sahbi [M]
To borrow	Istilaf, Isti'arah,
To look like / resemble	Yishbeh
Grandfather	Gid
To want	Awiz
To stay	Yifdal
To continue	Yikammil
Way (road, path)	Tari'
Way (method)	Tari'
I dont	Ana mesh, ana ma
To show	Yiwarri
To prepare	Yigahhiz
I am not going	Ana mish rayeh

Do you want to look like Salim
Inta Awiz tib'a shabah Salim?
I want to borrow this book for my grandfather
Ana awiz asta'ir ilkitab da ashan (or Li) giddi
I want to drive and to continue on this way to my house
Ana awiz asu' wa akammil ala il-tari' da lahaddi baiti
This isn't the way to do this
Di mish tari'at amal da?
I have a friend there, that's why I want to stay in Alexandria
Ana indi sahib hnak, ashan kida awiz afdal fil-Iskanderiyya
I am not going to see anyone here
Ana mish ha ashuf hadd hina
I need to show you how to prepare breakfast
Ana mihtag awarrik izzay tigahiz il fitar
Why don't you have the book?
Laih ma andaksh elkitab?
That is incorrect, I don't need the car today
Da mish sahih, ana mesh awiz il-arabeyah innahardah

*Sahih means "correct." However, *mish sahih* means "incorrect."
*Indak means "to have." "I have" is *ana andi*. However, "I don't have" is *ana ma'andish*.
*Lahaddi means "up to" or "to" as the final destination.
*In Egyptian Arabic, "to want" is *yi'uz*, "I want" is *awiz*, "he wants" is *awiz*, and she wants is *awzah*.

To remember	Aftikir
Your	Bita'ak/lik
Number	Nimrah
Hour	Sa'ah
Dark / darkness	Dalmah
About / on the	'An/ alal
Grandmother	Giddah
Five	Khamsa
Minute / Minutes	Di'i'ah/da'ayi'
More	Aktar
To think	Afakkar
To do	A'mil/Asawwi
To come	Agi
To hear	Asma'a
Last	Akhir
To talk / To Speak	Atkallem

You need to remember my number
Inta mihtag tiftikir nimriti
This is the last hour of darkness
Di akhir sa'at min il-dalmah
I want to come to hear my grandmother speak Arabic
Ana awiz agai asma'a gidditi titkallem Arabi
I need to think more about this, and what to do
Ana mihtag afakkar aktar fi dah, wi aih il-amal
From here to there, it's only five minutes
Il masafah min hina lahnak mugarrad khamsi da'a'yi'
The school on the mountain
Il madrassah alal gabal

Al masafa literally means "journey."

*In spoken Arabic "on" is *ala* and "the" is *al*. If I am to write it in Arabic, *ala* ("on") and *al* ("the") are separate, but because Egyptians make them sound like one word when they utter them, I joined the *ala* and *al* as one, and it became *alal*.

The Program

Early	Badri
To leave (to go)	Assib, yemshy
Again	Tani/marah tanyiah
Cairo	Qahera
To take	Akhud
To try	Agarrab
To rent	A'agar
Without her	Min ghairha
We are	Ihna
To turn off	Yi'fil
To ask	As'al
To stop	A'af
Permission	Izn
While	Fatra

He needs to leave and rent a house at the beach
Huwwa mihtag yissib wi yista'gir bait ala al bahr
We are here a long while
Ehna hina ba'alna fatra tawilah
I need to turn off the lights early tonight
Ana mihtag atfi innur badri illailah
We want to stop here
Ehna awzin no'af hina
We are from Cairo
Ihna min il-qahera
The same building
Il-imarah nafsaha
I want to ask permission to leave
Ana awiz atlub izn ashan assib

*In Egyptian Arabic, *ha'nib'a* gives the meaning that "we have been and will continue to be here for a long while." *Ha'nib'a*, literally speaking, means "will stay."
*In Egyptian Arabic, *ashan* means "because," but in Egyptian usage, it also simply means "to" and "in order to."

To open	Aftah
A bit, a little, a little bit	Shiwayyah
To pay	Adfa'a
Once again	Marrah taniah
There isn't/ there aren't	Ma fish, mish mawgud
Sister	Ukht
To hope	Atmanna
To live (to exist)	A'ish
To live (in a place)	Askun
Nice to meet you	Fursah sa'idah
Name	Ism
Last name	Ism il ailah
To return	Rugu'u [infinitive]/ Arga'a
Jerusalem	Il uds
Door	Bab/bawwabah

I need to open the door for my sister
Ana mihtag aftah il-bab li ukhti

I need to buy something
Mihtag ashtiri hagah

I want to meet your sisters
Awiz a'abil ekhwatak

Nice to meet you, what is your name and your last name
Fursah sa'idah, ismak wi ismi a'iltak aih?

To hope for a little better
Yitmanna hagah ahsan shiwayyah

I want to return to Qatar
Ana awiz Arga'a ala Qatar

I want to live 100 years
Ana awiz a'ish mit sanah

I need to return your book
Ana mihtag aragga'a kitabak

Why are you sad right now?
(M)Inta laih za'alan kidah dilwa'ti? (F) Inti laih za'alana kidah dilwa'ti?

There aren't any people here
Ma fish hadd hina

There isn't enough time to go to Jerusalem today
Ma fish wa'ti kafi aruh fih ala il-uds innahardah

*This *isn't* a phrase book! The purpose of this book is *solely* to provide you with the tools to create *your own* sentences!

To happen	Yigra/yihsal
To order	Yutlub/yu'mur
To drink	Yishrab
Excuse me	Lau samaht/ min fadlak
Child	(M)Walad, (F)bint
Woman	Sit
To begin / To start	Yibtidi
To finish	Yikhallas
To help	Yisa'id
To smoke	Yidakkhan
To love	Yihib
Afternoon	Ba'd idduhr

This must happen today
Dah lazim yihsal innahardah
Excuse me, my child is here with me as well
Min fadlak, ibni kaman ma'ayah hina
I love you
Bahibak
I see you
Ana shayfak
I need you at my side
Ana mihtag lak ganbi
I need to begin soon in order to be able to finish before 3 o'clock in the afternoon
Ana lazim abtidi bisur'ah ashan akhallas abli issa'ah talatah ba'd idduhr
I need help
Ana mihtag musa'dah
I don't want to smoke once again
Ana mish awiz adakkhan tani
I want to learn how to speak Arabic
Ana awiz at'allam izay atkallim Arabi

*"To help" is *asa'id*. However, "help!" is *mus'ada*. "I need help" or "I need rescue" / *ana mihtag mus'ada*.
*The definition of *ashan* is "in order to."

To read	Irayat [Infinitive], Yi'ra
To write	Kitabit [infinitive], Yiktib
To teach	Yidarris
To close	Yi'fil
To choose	Yikhtar
To prefer	Yifaddal
To put	Yihutt
Less	A'al
Sun	Shams
Month	Shahr
I Talk	Ana batkallam
Exact	Bezabt

I need this book in order to learn how to read and write in the Arabic language because I want to study in Egypt
Ana mihtag il-kitab dah ashan at'allam il-irayah wil kitabah billughah il-arabiah Ashan awiz adrus fi Masr

I want to close the door of the house
Ana awiz a'afil bawabit il-bait

I prefer to put the gift here
Ana afaddal ahutt il-hadiyyah hina

I want to pay less than you for the dinner
Ana awiz adfa'a a'alli minnak lil asha

I speak with the boy and the girl in French
Ana batkallam ma'a il walad wil bint bil faransawi

There is sun outside today
Il-shams barrah tal'ah innahardah

Is it possible to know the exact date?
Mumkin ni'raf il-tarikh bezabt?

*With the knowledge you've gained so far, now try to create your own sentences!

The Program

To exchange (*money*)	Sarf/tabdil omlah
To call	Ittisal
Brother	Akhu
Dad	Baba
To sit	A'a'ud
Together	Ma'a ba'd
To change	Yighayyir/yitghayyar
Of course	Tab'an, Ummal
Welcome	Ahlan
During	Ayyam, Wa'it
Years	Sanah/sinin
Sky	Sama
Up	Fu'u
Down	Taht
Sorry	Asif
To follow	Yilha'a
To the	Li
Big	Kibir
New	Gidid
Never / ever	Abadan, Umri ma

I don't want to exchange this money at the bank
Ana mish awiz abaddil il-omlah fil bank
I want to call my brother and my son today
Ana awiz attisil bi akhuyah wi ibni innahardah
Of course I can come to the theater, and I want to sit together with you and with your sister
Akid ha'adar agi il-masrah, wi awiz aa'ud ma'ak wi ma'a ukhtak
I need to go down to see your new house
Ana mihtag anzil ashan ashuf baitak il-gidid
I can see the sky from the window
Ana adir ashuf issama min il-shibbak
I am sorry, but he wants to follow her to the store
Ana assif, lakin huwwa awiz yilha'ha ala il mahil
I don't ever want to see you
Ana mish awiz ashufak abadan

*In Egyptian Arabic, "brother" is *akh*, and "dad" is *baba*. However, "my dad" is *babaya*, and "my brother" is *akhuya*. "My sister" is *ukhti*, and "my mother" is *mamti*.
*In the English language, the verb "to go down" isn't commonly used. However, in many foreign languages, the use of this verb is extremely prevalent.

To allow	Yismah
To believe	Yisadda'/yu'min
Morning	Sabah
Except	Illa
To promise	Yuu'id
Good night	Tisbah ala khair
To recognize	Yit'arraf ala
People	Ahl, nas, bani admin
To move (an object)	Yiharrik
To move (to a place)	Yen'el
Far	Bi'id
Different	Haga taniah
Man	Ragil
To enter	Yukhush/yudkhul
To receive	Yistilim
Pleasant	Latif/ Zarif
Good afternoon	Masa'a Al Khair
Left / right	Shimal/ Yimin
Him / Her	Huwwa/ Hiyya

I need to allow him to go with us, he is a different man now
Ana mihtag asmahluh yigi ma'ana, li'annuh etghayar wi ba'a insan tani dilwa'ti
I believe everything except this
Ana basadda'a kulli hagah illa da
I need to move the car because my sister needs to return home
Ana mihtag aharrik il-arabeyah ashan ukhti mihtagah tirga'a il-bait
I promise to say good night to my parents each night
Ana baw'id inni amassi ala mamti wi babaya kulli lailah
The people from Jordan are very pleasant
Il-urduniyin zarifin giddan
I need to find another hotel very quickly
Ana mihtag adawwar ala fundu' tani bisur'ah awi
They need to receive a book for work
Humma mihtagin yistilmu kitab lilshughl
I see the sun in the morning
Ana bashuf ilshams fil sabah
The house is on the right end of the street
Il-bait mawgud ala ilnahyah iltanyah min il-shari'i

*In Arabic, the article "the" is used when referring to countries, cities, or locations. "From Jordan" / *min al urdun.*

To wish	Yitmanna
Bad	Wihish
To Get	Yigib
To forget	Yinsa
Everybody / Everyone	Kulli wahid/ il-kul/gami'i innas
Although	Ma'a innuh
To feel	Yihis
Great	Azim
Next (following, after)	Gayyah/Adim
To like	Yi'gib
In front	Usad
Next (near, close)	Urayyib / ganb
Behind	Waraya
Well (as in doing well)	Kwayyis
Goodbye	Ma'a il salamah
Restaurant	Mat'am
Bathroom	Hammam

I don't want to wish you anything bad
Ana mish awiz atmannalak ayyi hagah wihshah
I must forget everybody from my past in order to feel well
Ana lazim ansa gami'i innas illi kanu fi hayati fil madi ashan ab'a kwayyis
I am next to the person behind you
Ana ganb ilshakhs illi warak
There is a great person in front of me
Fi shakhs azim uddami
Goodbye my friends
Ma'a is-salamah ya as-habi
Where is the bathroom in the restaurant?
Il-hamman fain fil mat'am?
She has to buy a car before the next year
Hiyya lazim tishtiri arabeyah abli il-sanah il-gayyah
I like the house, but it is very small
Il-bait agibni, bas huwwa sughayyar awi

*In Egyptian Arabic *Ab'a* means "to be" or "to become".

To remove / to take out	Yishil
Please	Min fadlak/ lau samaht
Beautiful	(M)Gamil, (F) Gamilah
To lift	Yirfa'a
Include / Including	Hasbana
Belong	Bita'a
To hold	Yimsik, yitmassak
To check	Ifhas
Small	Sughayyar
Real	Ha'i'i
Weather	El-gau
Size	Hagm, ma'as
High	Ali
Doesn't	Ma
So (as in then)	Yib'a
So (as in very)	Giddan, awi
Price	Il taman
Diamond	Massah

She wants to remove this door please
Hiyya awza tishil il-bab dah min fadlak
This week the weather was very beautiful
Il-usbu'u dah, il gau kan gamil awi
I need to know which is the real diamond
Ana mihtag a'araf ani fihum il al-massah il-ha'i'iyyah
We need to know the size of the house
Ihna mihtagin ni'rif hagm il-bait
I want to lift this, so you need to hold it high
Ana awiz arfa'a dah, ashan kidah inta mihtag timsikuh ali fu'u
I can pay this even though that the price is so expensive
Ana mumkin adfa'a il-mablagh dah ma' innuh ghali giddan
Including everything, is this price correct?
Iza hasabna kulli hagah, il-si'ir dah mazbut?

*In Arabic, the articles "this" and "that" become reversed when preceding a noun. "This" (*da*) "week" (*usbu'u*) becomes *usbu'u dah*.
*In Egyptian Arabic, *il-mablagh* means "the amount."

BUILDING BRIDGES

In Building Bridges, we take six conjugated verbs that have been selected after studies I have conducted for several months in order to determine which verbs are most commonly conjugated. For example, once you know how to say, "I need," "I want," "I can," and "I like," you will be able to connect words and say almost anything you want more correctly and understandably. The following three pages contain these six conjugated verbs in first, second, third, fourth, and fifth person, as well as some sample sentences. Please master the entire program up until here prior to venturing onto this section.

I want	Ana awiz
I need	Ana mihtag
I can	Ana a'adar, ana mumkin
I like	Ana yi'gibni
I go	Ana aruh
I have	Ana indi
I must / I have to	Ana lazim, Yajib alay

I want to go to my house
Ana awiz aruh baiti
I can go with you to the bus station
Ana mumkin aruh ma'ak mahattit il-utubis
I need to walk to the museum
Ana mihtag amshi lal mat-haf
I like to ride the train
Ana bahib rukub il-atr
I have to speak to my teacher
Ana lazim atkallam ma'a il-mudarrisah bita'ti
I have a book
Ana indi kitab

Please master pages #17-#39, prior to attempting the following pages!!

You want / do you want - Inta awiz/ Inta awiz?
He wants / does he want - Huwwa awiz/ huwwa awiz?
She wants / does she want - Hiyya awzah/ Hiyya awzah?
We want / do we want - Ihna awzin/ Ihna awzin?
They want / do they want - Humma awzin/Humma awzin?
You (plural) want - Intu awzin/ do you want? Awzin intu?

You need / do you need - Inta mihtag/ mihtag inta?
He needs / does he need - Huwwa mihtag/ mihtag huwwa?
She needs / does she need - Hiyya mihtagah/ mihtagah hiyya
We need / do we need - Ihna mihtagin/ mihtagin ihna?
They need / do they need - Humma mihtagin/mihtagin humma?
You (plural) need/ do you need? - Intu mihtagin/ Mihtagin intu?

You can / can you - Inta ti'dar/ti'dar inta?
He can / can he - Huwwa yi'dar/ yi'dar huwwa?
She can / can she - Hiyya ti'dar/ ti'dar hiyya?
We can / can we - Ihna ni'dar/ ni'dar ihna?
They can / can they - Humma yi'daru/ yi'daru humma?
You (plural) can - Intu ti'daru/ ti'daru intu, or intu ti'daru?

You like / do you like – Inta yi'gibak/ yi'gibak inta?
He likes / does he like – Huwwa yi'gibuh/ Yi'gibuh huwwa?
She like / does she like – Hiyya yi'gibha/ yi'gibha hiyya?
We like / do we like – Ihna yi'gibna/ Yi'gibna ihna?
They like / do they like – Humma yi'gibhum/ Yi'gibhum humma?
You (plural) like – Intu yi'gibkum/ Yi'gibkum intu?

You go / do you go - Inta bitruh/ Bitruh inta?
He goes / does he go - Huwwa biyruh/ Biyruh huwwa?
She goes / does she go - Hiyya bitruh/ Bitruh hiyya?
We go / do we go - Ihna binruh/ Binruh ihna?
They go / do they go – Humma biyruhu/ biyruhu humma?
You (plural) go/ do you go – Intu bitruhu/ bitruhu intu?

You have / do you have – Inta indak/ indak inta?
He has / does he have – Huwwa induh/ induh huwwa?
She has / does she have – Hiyya indaha/ indaha hiyya?
We have / do we have – Ihna indina/ ihna indina? Indina ihna?
They have / do they have – Humma induhum/ induhum humma?
You (plural) have/ do you have – Intu indukum/ indukum intu?

You must /must you? – Inta lazim/ lazim inta?
He must/ must he? – Huwwa lazim/Lazim huwwa?
She must/ must she –Hiyya lazmi/ Lazim hiyya?
We must/ must we? - Ihna lazim/lazim ihna?
They must / must they? – Humma lazim/ lazim humma?
You (plural) must/ must you? – Intu lazim/ Lazim intu?

Please master pages #17-#39, prior to attempting the following!!

Do you want to go?
Inta awiz tiruh?
Does he want to fly?
Huwwa awiz ytir?
We want to swim
Ihna awzin nisbah
Do they want to run?
Humma awzin yigru?
Do you need to clean?
Inta mihtag tinaddaf?
She needs to sing a song
Hiyya mihtaga tighanni ughniyah
We need to travel
Ihna mihtagin nisafir
They don't need to fight
Humma mish mihtagin yitkhan'u
You (plural) need to see
Intu mihtagin tishufu
Can you hear me?
Inta adir tisma'ni?
Yes, he can dance very well
Aywah, huwwa yi'dar yur'us kuwayyis awi
We can go out tonight
Ihna mumkin nukhrug il-lailah
They can break the wood
Humma yi'daru yikassiru il-khashab
Do you like to eat here?
Inta Bithib takul hina?

He likes to spend time here
Howa byheb ye'adi el wa'at hina
We like to fix the house
Ehna benheb tarteeb el beet
They like to cook
Huma beyhebbo el tabkh
You (plural) like my house
Howa intu a'agibkom beeti?
Do you go to school today
Hal betrooh il madrasah enaharda?
He goes fishing
Howa byrooh leystad samak
We are going to relax
Ahna rooh nestarkhi
They go to watch a film
Homa byroho yitfarago ala film
Do you have money?
Hal ma'ak felous?
She must look outside
Lazim tebos bara
We have to sign our names
Lazem nuwaka be asameena
They have to send the letter
Lazim neba-at il resalah
You (plural) have to order
Into lazim tetlobo

Countries of the Middle East
Dual il-shar'i il-awsat

Lebanon	Libnan
Syria	Surya
Jordan	Il-urdun
Israel/Palestine/West Bank	Isra'il/Falastin/il-diffah il-gharbiyyah
Iraq	Il-Ira'a
Saudi Arabia	Il-Suudiyah
Kuwait	Il-Kuwait
Qatar	Qatar
Bahrain	Il-Bahrain
United Arab Emirates	Il-Imarat
Oman	Uman
Yemen	Yaman
Egypt	Masr
Libya	Libya
Tunisia	Tunis
Algeria	Il-Gaza'ir
Morocco	Il-Maghrib

Months

January	Yunayir
February	Fibrayir
March	Mars
April	Ibril
May	Mayu
June	Yunyu
July	Yuliu
August	Aughustus
September	Sebtamber
October	Uktubar
November	Nufambr
December	Disambr

Days of the Week

Sunday	Yum al-ahadd
Monday	Yum al-itnin
Tuesday	Yum al-talat
Wednesday	Yum al-'arb'a
Thursday	Yum al-khamis
Friday	Yum al-gom'a
Saturday	Yum is-sabt

Seasons

Spring	Rabi'i
Summer	Saif
Autumn	Kharif
Winter	Shita

Cardinal Directions

North	Shimal
South	Gunub
East	Sharq
West	Gharb

Colors

Black	(M)Aswad (F)Suda
White	(M)Abyad (F)Baida
Gray	(M)Ramadi (F)Ramadiyyah
Red	(M)Ahmar (F)Hamra
Blue	(M)Azra' (F)Zar'a
Yellow	(M)Asfar (F)Safra
Green	(M)Akhdar (F)Khadra
Orange	(M)Burtu'ani/(F)Burtu'aniyyah
Purple	(M)Banafsigi/(F)Banafsigiyyah
Brown	(M)Bunni (F)Bunniyyah

Numbers

One	Wahd
Two	Itnain
Three	Talata
Four	Arba'a
Five	Khamsa
Six	Sitta
Seven	Sab'a
Eight	Tamanya
Nine	Tis'a
Ten	Ashara

Twenty	Ishrin
Thirty	Talatin
Forty	Arb'in
Fifty	Khamsin
Sixty	Sittin
Seventy	Sab'in
Eighty	Tamanin
Ninety	Tis'in
Hundred	Miyya
Thousand	Alif
Million	Malyun

Conversational Arabic
Quick and Easy

LIBYAN DIALECT

YATIR NITZANY

Libyan Arabic

Libyan Arabic, also known as Libyan Vernacular Arabic or Sulaimitian Arabic, is a variety of Arabic spoken in Libya and its neighboring countries, Egypt and Niger. It is the dialect of Tripoli and a widespread language used especially in the north of the country. Two major historical events have shaped the Libyan dialect: the Hilalian-Sulaimi migration and the migration of Arabs from Muslim Spain to North Africa following the Reconquista. Most of the vocabulary in Libyan Arabic is of Classical Arabic origin, usually with a modified interconsonantal vowel structure. Many Italian loanwords also exist because of Libya's colonial past, in addition to Turkish, Berber, Spanish, and English words. The bulk of vocabulary in Libyan Arabic has the same meaning as in Classical Arabic; however, many words have different but related meanings. Nouns in Libyan Arabic are marked for two genders (masculine and feminine) and three numbers (singular, dual, and plural). It is estimated that around 3.2 million people speak the language in Libya and that there are over 3.5 million speakers all over the world in total. Libyan Arabic is not considered an official language but is taught at schools and used in poetry and cultural documents; it is also used on TV and radio, folk songs, cartoons, and by people on emails and social media.

Spoken in: Libya

ARABIC PRONUNCIATIONS

PLEASE MASTER THE FOLLOWING PAGE IN ARABIC PRONUNCIATIONS PRIOR TO STARTING THE PROGRAM

Kha. For Middle Eastern languages including Arabic, Hebrew, Farsi, Pashto, Urdu, Hindi, etc., and also German, to properly pronounce the kh or ch is essential, for example, *Khaled* (a Muslim name) or *Chanukah* (a Jewish holiday) or *Nacht* ("night" in German). The best way to describe kh or ch is to say "ka" or "ha" while at the same time putting your tongue at the back of your throat and blowing air. It's pronounced similarly to the sound that you make when clearing your throat. Please remember this whenever you come across any word containing a kh in this program.

Ghayin. The Arabic gh is equivalent to the "g" in English, but its pronunciation more closely resembles the French "r," rather than "g." Pronounce it at the back of your throat. The sound is equivalent to what you would make when gargling water. Gha is pronounced more as "rha," rather than as "ga." *Ghada* is pronounced as "rhada." In this program, the symbol for *ghayin* is gh, so keep your eyes peeled.

Aayin is pronounced as a'a, pronounced deep at the back of your throat. Rather similar to the sound one would make when gagging. In the program, the symbol for *aayin* is a'a, u'u, o'o, or i'i. In this program "3" will be occasionally used to signify *aayin*.

Ha is pronounced as "ha." Pronunciation takes place deep at the back of your throat, and for correct pronunciation, one must constrict the back of the throat and exhale air while simultaneously saying "ha." In the program, this strong h ("ha") is emphasized whenever *ha, ah, hi, he,* or *hu* is encountered. In this program "7" will be occasionally used to signify *ha.*

*The use of numerical symbols to identify Arabic accents is known as the Franco-Arabic technique, in which "3" is used to signify *aayin,* "7" is used to signify *ha,* "3'" (with an apostrophe after the numeral) is used to signify *ghayin,* and "5" to signify *kha.* However, in this program we will solely be using the numerical digits of "3" and "7."

NOTE TO THE READER

The purpose of this book is merely to enable you to communicate in the Libyan Arabic dialect. In the program itself (pages 17-38) you may notice that the composition of some of those sentences might sound rather clumsy. This is intentional. These sentences were formulated in a specific way to serve two purposes: to facilitate the easy memorization of the vocabulary and to teach you how to combine the words in order to form your own sentences for quick and easy communication, rather than making complete literal sense in the English language. So keep in mind that this is not a phrase book!

As the title suggests, the sole purpose of this program is for conversational use only. It is based on the mirror translation technique. These sentences, as well as the translations are not incorrect, just a little clumsy. Latin languages, Semitic languages, and Anglo-Germanic languages, as well as a few others, are compatible with the mirror translation technique.

Many users say that this method surpasses any other known language learning technique that is currently out there on the market. Just stick with the program and you will achieve wonders!

Note to the Reader

Again, I wish to stress this program is by no means, shape, or form a phrase book! The sole purpose of this book is to give you a fundamental platform to enable you to connect certain words to become conversational. Please also read the "Introduction" and the "About Me" section prior to commencing the program.

In order to succeed with my method, please start on the very first page of the program and fully master one page at a time prior to proceeding to the next. Otherwise, you will overwhelm yourself and fail. Please do not skip pages, nor start from the middle of the book.

It is a myth that certain people are born with the talent to learn a language, and this book disproves that myth. With this method, anyone can learn a foreign language as long as he or she follows these explicit directions:

* Memorize the vocabulary on each page

* Follow that memorization by using a notecard to cover the words you have just memorized and test yourself.

* Then read the sentences following that are created from the vocabulary bank that you just mastered.

* Once fully memorized, give yourself the green light to proceed to the next page.

Again, if you proceed to the following page without mastering the previous, you are guaranteed to gain nothing from this book. If you follow the prescribed steps, you will realize just how effective and simplistic this method is.

The Program

Let's Begin! "Vocabulary" (Memorize the Vocabulary)

I | I am - Aneey
With you - Ma'ak / ma'ak "used for both"
With him / with her - Ma'ah / ma'aaha
With us - Ma'na
For you - (**Masc**)Leek / (**Fem**) leek "used for both"
Without him – Min ghayrah
Without them – Min ghayrhoom
Always – Dema
Was - Kan
This, This is - (Masc) Hada/ (Fem) hadey
Today - El yom
Sometimes - Ahyanan
Maybe - Maraat / momken
Tripoli – Trabless
Better - Ahsan/afdal
You, you are, are you - (M)enta / (F) enti
You (plural) - Entom
He / she - Howwa /Heyya
From - Min

I am with you
Aneey ma'k
This is for you
Hada leek
But for more than one person (hada leykom)
I am from Libya
Aneey min Leebya
Are you from Tripoli?
(Masc) Enta min trabless
(Fem) Inti min trabless
Sometimes you are with us at the mall
maraat enta maa'ana fe el mol
(F) maraaat inti maa'ana fe el mol
I am always with her
Aney deyma ma3aha
Are you without them today?
Enta min ghayrhoom el yom
(F) Inta min ghayrhoom el yom
Sometimes I am with him
Maraat ankoon ma'u

---

*In Arabic, there are gender rules. The masculine case for "for you" is *laka*; the feminine case is *laki*. The endings of *–ka* and *–ki* are used quite often in the Arabic language to signify gender.

*Mall can also be said *mall* in the Libyan dialect. It can be *soog*.

I was - Aney konet
To be - (M)Ykun / (F) Tkun
The - Al
Same - Nafasah / zayah
Good - Emlee7 / kwayyes bahie
Here – Ahney
Very – Haalba
And - Wa
Between - Beyn
Now - Tawa
Later / after / afterwards - Ba'aden
If - Law
Yes - Eyh / na3am
To - Mesh
Tomorrow - Ghodwa / bukra
Person - Shakhs / wahed
Also / too / as well - Hata, hata howa

It's better tomorrow
Ahsan ghodwa ghodwa ahsan
This is good as well
Hata hada a7sen hata hada bahei
To be the same person
Mesh eykon nafs elshakhs
Yes, you are very good
Eh, enta ekwayes halbaa
I was here with them
Aneey kent maaom
You and I
Enta wa aney
The same day
Nafs elyoum

*The use of numerical symbols to identify Arabic accents is known as the Franco-Arabic technique, in which "3" is used to signify *aayin*, "7" is used to signify *ha*, "3'" (with an apostrophe after the numeral) is used to signify *ghayin*, and "5" to signify *kha*. However, in this program we will solely be using the numerical digits of "3" and "7."

*In the Arabic language, adjectives follow the noun. For example, "the same day" is *nafs el youm*, small house" is *beit zgheer/ hosh asgheer*, "tall person" is *shakhs tawil*, and "short person" is *shakhs aseer*.

*In this program, the article "the" (*al*) will sometimes become a prefix at the beginning of the noun. For nouns beginning with *d, n, r, s, sh, t, th*, and *z* the *l* is omitted and replaced with the initial consonant of the following noun. "The people" / *al-shakhs is ashakhs*. "The Nile" / *al-nil is an-nil*. It is dropped when spoken; however, when written, it's usually al-shaks or al-nil.

*In Libyan Arabic, *ghodwa* and *bukra* are used to signify "tomorrow." However, in the case of the Tripoli dialect, *ghodwa* is more commonly used than *bukra*.

Me – Read footnote
Ok – Ayh /bahie
Even if - Hatta iza/ hatta law
No - La'
Worse - Aswa'
Where - Waen
Everything - Kolsshay/ holhen
Somewhere - Fe makan/mo3ayen
What - Shenow
Almost - Tagrieban / egrayeb
There - Ghadika / ghadi

Afterwards is worse
Ba'dha aswa'
Even if I go now
Hata law 'meshaaet tawa
Where is everything?
Weyn kel shi?
Maybe somewhere
Marat fe makan mo'yen
What? I am almost there
Shenow? aney egrayeb ghadi
Where are you?
Weynak?

*Fi mekan literally means in a place.

*In Libyan Arabic, the pronoun "me" has several definitions. In relation to verbs it's *neh* or *leh*. *Leh* refers to any verb that relates to the action of doing something to someone or for someone.
For example,
"tell me" / *goly aney*, "tell (to) me" / *goly*.
Ni just means "me": "love me" / *heb nee* or "see me" / *shoofnee*.
Other variations (*yeh, eh*):
*"on me" / *'aleyyeh*, "in me" / *fiyyeh*, "to me" / *leyah*,
*"in front of me" / *gidaamy*, "from me" / *minnehy*
The same rule applies for "him" and "her"; both become suffixes; *o* and *a*. Basically all verbs pertinent to male end with *o* and all pertinent to female end with *a*).
*"love her" / *hebaha*, "love him" / *heba*
*"love them" / *hebhom*, "love us" / *hebnah*
Any verb that relates to doing something to someone, for someone put *l*:
*"tell her" / *goli liha*, "tell him" / *gol la'howa*
*"tell them" / *goli lhom*, "tell us" / *goli lnehney*
Adding you as a suffix in Arabic is *ak* or *lak*, female *ik* or *lik*.
*"love you" / *enhebak, enhibik*
*"tell you" / *engolak, engolik*

*In Libyan Arabic, we use *umrak? / umrek* to signify the male and female case of "how old are you?" However, another common form of saying it is (M) *gidash 3omrak* (or) *kam 3omrak* / (F) *gidash 3omrek* (or) *gidash omrek*.

House - Hosh
In / at - Fi /bel /be
Car - Sayyarah
Already - Hala
Good morning - Sabah el-kheyr
How are you? - (M)Kif halak or shen eljaw / (F)kif halek?
Where are you from? - (M)Min weyn enta?/(F)Min weyn Inti?
Today - Elyoum
Hello - Marhaba
What is your name? - (M)Shenow esmak(F)Shou smik/shenow esmek
How old are you? - (M)Gadaash Umrak? / (F) Gadaash Umrek?
Son - Weldi
Daughter - Benti
To have - Mesh ykoon andy
Doesn't *(or)* **isn't** - (M)(F)(for adjectives) Mo / (for verbs) mish
Hard - Sa'ab
Still - Mazal / ga'da
So (as in then) - Badahaa/faa

She doesn't have a car, maybe she is still at the house
Heyya ma'endhash seyyarah ma'naha marat ga'da fe elhosh
I am in the car already with your son and daughter
Aney fe elsayyarah ma'a bintak wa wildak
Good morning, how are you today?
Sabaah elkhyeer keef halak elyom?
Hello, what is your name?
Marhaba, sheen esmak?
How old are you?
Gidash omrak or kam omrak?
This is very hard, but it's not impossible
Hady sa'ba laken mish mosta7il
Where are you from?
Min weyn m. enta / f. inti?

*In Arabic, possessive pronouns become suffixes to the noun. For example, in the translation for "your," *ak* is the masculine form, and *ik* is the feminine form.
- "your book" / *katabak* (m.), *katabik* (f.)
- "your house" / *beetak* (m.), *beetek* (f.)
*In the Arabic language, as well as in other Semitic languages, the article "a" doesn't exist. "She doesn't have a car" / *hiyya ma a'anda sayyarah*.

Thank you – Shookraan
For - Ala khater /lil/li
Anything - Ayya haja /ayya shi
That / That is - (M)Hadaka, ahowa (F)hadika, hadiy
Time - Waget
But - Laken
No / not - *(adjectives)* Mo / *(verbs)* mish
I am not - Aney mish
Away - B'eed
Late - Meta'akhir
Similar - Yeshbah / zaya
Another/ other - Tani/ shi tani
Side - Janab
Until – La/ laen
Yesterday - Embareh / ames
Without us - Min gherna
Since - Min
Day - Yom
Before – Gabel

Thanks for anything
Shukran ala Ayya Shi
It's almost time
Egreeb alwaget/garaab alwaget
I am not here, I am away
Aney mish hena, aney b'eyd
That is a similar house
Hada nafs elhosh
I am from the other side
Aney min eljeyha el tanya or aney min el taraf eltani
But I was here until late yesterday
Laken aney konet hena la waget met'agher embareh
I am not at the other house
Aney mish fe el7osh eltani

In Libyan Arabic, there are three definitions for time:
* "time" / *waget* refers to "era", "moment period," "duration of time."
* "time(s)" / *marra(t)* refers to "occasion" or "frequency."
* "time" / *sa'a* references "hour," "what time is it?"

*In Libyan Arabic, *mo* and *mish* are used to define "no," "not," "isn't," "doesn't," and "don't." However, we use mo regarding cases of adjectives and mish to define cases of verbs.

What time is it? - Gidash el saa3a?/ esa'a kam?
I say / I am saying - Aney engol
I want - Nebe
Without you - (M) Minghirak/ (F) minghirek
Everywhere/wherever - Fe kol emkan / wein ma tkoon
I go, I am going - (M)Aney mashy /(F)aney mashya
With - Ma'a
My – (read footnote)
Cousin - (M)Wild 3ami(or) wild khali [uncle from mother's side], (F)Bent al'am/ Bent alkhal, (plural) saghaar aami
I need - Aney mehtaj / lazim
Right now - Tawa / haleyan
Night - Leyl/ masa
To see - Mesh etshof
Light - Dhau /dhay
Outside - Barra
Without - Bidoun/bila/minghir
Happy - Farhan/sa'aeed
I see / I am seeing - Aney enshouf
I am saying no / I say no
Aney engol la
I want to see this today
(M) nebi en shofah el yom /(F)nebi enshofha elyom
I am with you everywhere
Aneey ma'ak fi kulli makan
I am happy without my cousins here
(M)Aney far7an min ghir saghaar aami hena
I need to be there at night
Lazim enkoun ghadi fe elleyl
I am seeing light outside
Aney enshouf fe dhay barra
What time is it right now?
Gidash el saa3a tawa

---

*"Mine" / *leyah* is also a possessive pronoun. *Ebta'y* means "my" but also becomes a suffix to a noun. Nouns ending in a vowel end with –*teh*. However, nouns ending with a consonant end with –*eh*. For example:

- "cousin" / *weld al'am*, "my cousin" / *weld 'amei*. * "cup" / *tasah*, "my cup" / *tastyeh*

For second and third person masculine noun, *weld* ("son"), male (*ak*) male plural (*kom*) and female (*ik*) female plural (*kum*). For example: "your son" / *weldak* (m.), *weldik* (f.), "your (plural) son" /*weldkom* (m.), *bintkom* (f.), "his son" / *weldah*, "her son" / *weldaha*, "our son" / *weldnah*, "their son" / *weldhom* (m.), *binthom* (f.) For second and third person feminine noun: "car" / *seyyara*. For example: "your car" / *seyyartak*, "your (plural) car" / *seyyaretkom*, *seyyaretkum*, "his car" / *seyyatah*, "her car" / *seyyaretaha*, "our car" / *seyyaretna*, "their car" / *seyaret hom* (m.), *seyyaret hen* (f.)

*In Libyan Arabic *lazim* means "must", however both will be used interchangeably to represent the verb "need".

***This *isn't* a phrase book! The purpose of this book is *solely* to provide you with the tools to create *your own* sentences!**

Place - Makan
Easy - Sahel
To find - Mesh taalgaa
To look for/to search - Mesh edawwer
Near / Close - Egreeb
To wait - Mesh Ystanna / mesh etrajy
To sell - Mesh etbeea
To use - Yesta'amil
To know - Mesh taaref/mesh naaref (if you are speaking about yourself)
To decide - Mesh nkaarer
Between - Beyn
Both - Azoz
To - A'al / Lil- "prefix"
Next to - Bahdah / bejaneb

This place is easy to find
Saahel taalgah almkan hada
I want to look for this next to the car
Nebi endaweer 3ala hada ba7da elsyyarah
I am saying to wait until tomorrow
Aney engoul nestanow la ghodwa
This table is easy to sell
Haady el tawla sahel tenba3
I want to use this
Nebi nesta3mel hady
I need to know where is the house
Nebi ne'ref weyn elhosh
I want to decide between both places
Nebi nakhtaar beyen alhayash azoz

*In Libyan Arabic *mesh* means "to" or "in order to" and sometimes "because" as well. "To go, you have to use a car" / *mesh trooh, lazem testa'mel sayara.*

Because - 'Ala khater / leanna
To buy - Mesh neshree/tshree (if you are referring to someone else)
Sea - Bahir
Them | they | their - Homa
Bottle - Sheeshet
Book - Ktab
Mine - Leyah
To understand - Mesh nafham
Problem / Problems - (S) Moshkla / (P) Mashehkill
I do / I am doing - Aney andeer
Of - 'Mtaa 'I think"
To look – Mesh nshoof
Myself - Brohe
Enough - Khalas / saad/yaaser
Food / water - Akill *(or)* makla / emmayeh
Each/ every/ entire/ all - Kol
Hotel - Fondok/hotel

I like this hotel because I want to look at the sea
Aney ajabani elfondok hada ala khatir nebe netfara aly el bahir
I want to buy a bottle of water
Nebe neshrey sheeshet emmaya
I do this every day
Aney nedeer feeh kol yom
Both of them have enough food
Homa el zoz 3endhom makla tsedhom
That is the book, and that book is mine
Had huwweh el ketab, w had el ketab leyah
I need to understand the problem
Aney nebi nafham el moshkla
I see the view of the city from the hotel
Aney enshoof fe mandar el madina min el fondok
I do my homework today
Endeer fe wajby el yom
My entire life (all my life)
Kol hayaty

*"At the" is *el*.
*"Both of them" is *homa el zoz*.
*There are two ways of saying "life" in Arabic: *'omr* and *hayaaty*.
**Enheb* is "to love," but when you say, "I like this place," for example, we say, *ana habit el makan*.

I like - Enheb
There is / There are - Fe
Family / Parents - Omwaleyah/ boy w omy
Why - 'Alash / Khyeerk
To say - Mesh engool
Something - Haja
To go - Mesh temshy
Ready - Mesh waaty /newaty means (I am going to make this "x" ready)
Soon - Greeb
To work - Mesh nekhdim
Who - Shkon / meno
To know - Mesh naaref/mesh taaref
That *(conjunction)* **-** Inna / maadee
There - Ghadeeka/ghady/hnak

I like to be at my house with my parents
Enheb nkoon fi elhosh/hooshe ma' boy w omy
I want to know why I need to say something important
Nebe ne'ref 'alash aney mihtaj engool haja mohema
I am there with him
Aneey ghadeeka ma3ah
I am busy, but I need to be ready soon
Aney mashghool, laaken lazem ankoon waty fe agraab waget
I like to go to work
Enheb en3ady lil khidma / enheb nemshey lil khidma
'Who is there?
Menow ghady?
I want to know if they are here, because I want to go outside
nebe ne'ref law homa hena, 'ala khater nebe nemshy la-barra
There are seven dolls
Fe saba' lei'aab
I need to know that that is a good idea
Lazem naraf inna hady fekra bahya/kwesa

*In the last sentence, we use "that" as a conjunction (*inna*) and a demonstrative pronoun (*haady*).

How much /how many - Gedaash
To bring – Enjeeb
With me - M'aay
Instead – Badel
Only - Bas
When - Lama/ emta?
I can / Can I? - Aney nagder / nagder aney?
Or - Walah
Were - Kan
Without me - Min ghayre anay
Fast - Bsor'aah
Slow - Batee'
Cold - Sagaa'
Inside - Dakhel
To eat - Bnakel
Hot – Naww

How much money do I need to bring with me?
Gedaash floos aney mehtaj njeeb ma'aay?
Instead of this cake, I want that cake
Bedal hady el kyka, nebe el kyka hady
Only when you can
Bas lamma tagder
They were without me yesterday
Homa kano min ghayree ammes
Do I need to drive the car fast or slow?
Nsoog aleyyra bosoraa walaa beshwaaya
It is cold inside the library
Sag'a dakhel el maktabe
Yes, I like to eat this hot for my lunch
Ewya, aney neheb nakel el akl skhoon fel ghadey
I can work today
Aney nagdir nekhdem elyoum

*"Were" is *kano*, but for "they were". "We were" is *konna*.

*"I can" is *aney nagdir* and *"can I?"* is *nagder aney?* "You can" or "can you?" is *enta tagdir*.

To answer - Mesh enjaweb
To fly - Benteer / Mesh entaeer
Time / times - Marra/Marrat
To travel - Mesh ensafer
To learn - Mesh netaalem
How - Keef
To swim - Mesh enoom
To practice - Mesh netmarin
To play - Mesh nal 3ab
To leave *(an object)* **-** Beysh inkhaly
Many /much /a lot - Halba
I go to - 'Anay nemshe le
First - Al awal
To leave *(to go)* **-** Beysh nemshy

I want to answer many questions
Nebe enjawib 'ala halba as'ela
I must fly to Dubai today
Lazem nteer le dubai elyoum
I need to learn how to swim at the pool
Aney nebe net'alem keef en'oom fe 7od el sebaha
I want to learn to play better tennis
Nebe net'alem nel'aab tennis ahsen
I want to leave this here for you when I go to travel the world
Hada minkhli''hoolek ahney lama nemshe nesafaar hwaol alalem
Since the first time
Men awal marra
The children are yours
Haadom asghaarek

*In Libyan Arabic, "to leave (something)" is *beysh inkhaly*. "To leave (a place)" is *beysh nemshy*.

***With the knowledge you've gained so far, now try to create your own sentences!**

Nobody / anyone - Mafee had/ay had
Against - Dud
Us - Nahna
To visit - Ti'zor
Mom / Mother - Mama, em
To give - Taa'ti
Which - Ayy
To meet - Mesh netlaaga
Someone - Wahad
Just - Bas
To walk – Mesh nemshey
Around - Hawl
Towards - Be etejah/jeehet
Than - Min
Nothing – La'shai/wala haja

Something is better than nothing
Haja khayer min la'shai
I am against him
Aney dedda howa
Is there anyone here?
Fee haad aheny
We go to visit my family each week
Nehna en3ado nezooro fe omwaleya kol osboo3 / aheny nemshoo le aayalti kool osbooaha
I need to give you something
Ane mihtaj ne'teek haja / naabi naateek haja
Do you want to go meet someone?
Tebe et'ady etshoof wa7ed / tebe taamshey tshoof haad
I was here on Wednesdays as well
Aney konet hena hata yom el arbe'
Do you do this everyday?
Enta etdeer fe hada kol yom
You need to walk around, but not towards the house
Enta lazem edeer dora lakin mish tejah el hosh

---

*In Arabic, when using the pronoun "you" as a direct and indirect object pronoun (the person who is actually affected by the action that is being carried out) in relation to a verb, the pronoun *"you"* becomes a suffix to that verb. That suffix becomes *ak* (masc.) *ik* (fem.).
- "to give" / *ta'teh*: "to give you" / *ta a'teek*
- "to tell" / *etgol*: "to tell you" / *eygolak* (m.), *eygolik* (f.)
- "see you" / *enshoofak*: "to see you" (plural) / *enshookom* (m.), *enshookin* (f.) For third person male, add *hu* (*hum*, plural), for female *ha* (*hu'nn*, plural).

I have - Andi
Don't - Ma
Friend - Saheb, sadi
To borrow – Netsaalf
To look like / resemble – Yashebah
Like (preposition) **-** Zay
Grandfather - Jedi
To want – Mesh nabi
To stay - Mesh noogoad
To continue – Mesh nkamel
Way - Tari / droub
I don't – Ma
To show – Mesh noarey
To prepare – Mesh nowaty
I am not going - Manish mashe
Correct - Mazboot
Incorrect - Mish sa7 / ghalat

Do you want to look like Salim
Tebe teshbah saleem?
I want to borrow this book for my grandfather
Nebe nest'eer el ketab hada le jeddi
I want to drive and to continue on this way to my house
Aney nebe ensoog wa enkamil eltereeg hady li hoshy
I have a friend there, that's why I want to stay in Sirt
'Endy sahbe ghady hada 'alash nebe nog'od fe seert
I am not going to see anyone here
Aney mish hanshoof had hena
I need to show you how to prepare breakfast
Aney lazem en wareek keef etdeer el fotor
Why don't you have the book?
'Alash ma 'andak el ketab?
That is incorrect, I don't need the car today
Hada mish sa7 aney mish mehtaj el sayyarah el yom

To remember - Mesh tiddaker
Your - Leek
Number - Ragm
Hour - Se'a'a
Dark / darkness - Emathlem/ thalam
About / on the - 'Mesh/ ala
Grandmother - Henay
Five - Khamsa
Minute / minutes - Dgeega/ dgayg
More - Aktar
To think - Mesh etfakir
To do - Ndeer / Mesh endeer
To come - Mesh enjee
To hear - Mesh nama3
Last - Akher

You need to remember my number
Enta mihtaj teddakar ragmy
This is the last hour of darkness
Haade akher sa'a men el thalam
I want to come and to hear my grandmother speak Arabic
Aney nebe neje w nesmaa' henay tetkalam 'araby
I need to think more about this, and what to do
Aney mihtaj nfakkar aktar fe haada, wa keef ndeer
From here to there, it's only five minutes
Min hena le ghady khamsa digayg bas
The school on the mountain
El madrase 'ala el jabal
Where is the embassy
Waen el safara
Where is the hospital
Waen al mostshafa
I want to sleep
Ahney nabi noorged

Beach - Shat
Again - 'Maraa tanyaa /awed (also used in a different manner)
He needs - Howa mihtaj
To take – Mesh nakhed/takhed (used when referring to someone else)
To try - 'etjareeb
To rent – Mesh N'ajer
Without her - Min kherha / min ghayerha heya
We are - E7nee
To turn off - Mesh etafee
To ask - Mesh tasael
To stop - Mesh enwagef
Permission - Eden

He needs to leave and rent a house at the beach
Howa laazem yemshy wa ey ajer hosh ala el shat
I want to take the test without her
Aabi endeer el emtehan min ghayrha
We are here a long time
Lenaa halbaa ahnaey/ahnaey henay lenaa waget
I need to turn off the lights early tonight
Ane mihtaj ntaffee el daw bakry el leela
We want to stop here
Ehney nebo enwagfo hena
We are from Tripoli
Ahnaey min trabless
The same building
Nafs el mabna
I want to ask permission to leave
Nebi notlob eden mesh natlaa

*In Libyan Arabic *atlaa* means "to go out."

*In Libyan Arabic "to stop" is *nwagef,* but to cease" is *khalas*. For example, if someone is bothering you, you tell them STOP! / *khalas*.

*In Libyan Arabic, when one is speaking about oneself, one sometimes attaches an *n* before the verb. Example: "Rent" is *ajer*, but "I will rent" is *ane n'ajer*.

To open - Mesh naftah
A bit, a little, a little bit - Eshwaya
To pay - Mesh taadfaah
Once again - Marra tanya
There isn't/ there aren't - Ma feesh
Sister - Okht
To hope - Mesh titmana
To live - Mesh taeesh
Nice to meet you - Tsharrafna bma'riftak
Name - Ism
Last name - Ism el 3aela
To return - Mesh towaly
Sad – Haazen
Door - Bab

I need to open the door for my sister
Lazem neftah el baab le okhty
I need to buy something
Lazem neshery haja
I want to meet your sisters
Nebe nagaabel khawatek
Nice to meet you, what is your name and your last name?
Tsharrafna bma'riftak (female bma'riftik), sheno esmak w esm el 3aela?
To hope for a little better
Mesh netmanno/netmanna ahsen beshwaya
I want to return from the United States and to live in Qatar without problems
Ane nebe nerja' mn amerika w n'eesh fe Qatar bala mashkal
Why are you sad right now?
'Alash ente hazeen tawa? Khayrek horjaan tawa
There aren't any people here
Mafeesh ay haed ahnay
There isn't enough time to go to Benghazi today
Mafeesh waget ey sid beash nimsho le baneghazi elyoum

*In Libyan Arabic, regarding the verb "to meet," there are two separate cases to define this verb: *tejtehme'* and *tgaabel*, depending of the context. To meet for business is *tejtehme'*. To meet for getting acquainted is *tgaabel*. In the sentence, "Do you want to go meet someone?" (the sister, getting acquainted with her), it's *tgaabel*.
**Mesh saad* means "insufficient."
*This *isn't* a phrase book! The purpose of this book is *solely* to provide you with the tools to create *your own* sentences!

To happen - Mesh ey seer
To order - Mesh totlob
To drink - Mesh tashrob
Excuse me - 'Afwan / ba'ad idnak
Child - Wild
Woman - Emr'ah
To begin / to start - Mesh tabda'
To finish - Mesh eytem
To help - Mesh ey sa'ed
To smoke - Mesh edakhin
To love - Mesh et heb
To talk / to speak - Mesh titkalim

This must happen today
Haad lazem yaseer elyoum
Excuse me, my child is here as well
'Afwan wildy hata howa ahenay
I love you
An'haabek
I see you
Aney nshoof feek
I need you at my side
Aney mahatajek tkoon jamby
I need to begin soon to be able to finish at 3 o'clock in the afternoon
Aney mihtaj nebda' 'egrayeb 'ala khater entim esa'a 3 ba'ad el dohr
I need help
Aney mihtaj mosaa'da
I don't want to smoke once again
Aney ma nebeysh endakhen marra tanya
I want to learn how to speak Arabic
Aney nebe net'allem netkalem 'araby

*"To help" is *sa'ed*. However, "help!" is *museh'adeh*. "I need help" or "I need rescue" / *aneey meh'teij musa'da*.

*"To be able to" is *mesh naekdar*

To read - Mesh taggra
To write - Mesh tekteb
To teach - Mesh et'aalem
To close - Mesh itsakir
To choose - Mesh tekhtaar
To prefer - Mesh etfadil
To put - Mesh ot-hot
Less - Agael
Sun - Shames
Month - Shaher
I talk - Aney netkalem
Exact - Masbot /bezaabt

I need this book to learn how to read and write in Arabic because I want to teach in Egypt
Ane mihtaj el ketab hada net'alem el geraya wel ketaba bel 'araby 'lanaa nebe engary fe masrr
I want to close the door of the house
Ane nebe nsakker baab el 7osh
I prefer to put the gift here
Ane enfadil in 7ot el hdeye ahney
I want to pay less than you for the dinner
Ane nebe nedfaa' agal menak aly elasha
I speak with the boy and the girl in French
Ane bnetkalem ma' el walad wel bent bel faransi
There is sun outside today
Fi shamess baraa elyoum
Is it possible to know the exact date?
Mumken ne'raf el tareekh bezaabt?

To exchange (*money*) - Mesh ensaarf
To call - Mesh nkalem
Brother – Khoy
Dad – Booy
To sit - Gaa'mez
Together - Maa' baa'dna
To change - Mesh nghayr
Of course – Akeed
Welcome - Ahlan/ahleen
During – Mabaen
Years - (S)Seneh / (P)esneen
Sky – Elsmae
Up – Fog
Down – Lota
Sorry – Aseef
To follow - Mesh tatba'
To the – Lil
Big – Ekbeer
New – Ejdid
Never / ever – Abdaa/abad

I don't want to exchange this money at the bank
Aney ma nebesh en saref el flos fe elbank
I want to call my brother and my dad today
Ane nebe ntsaal ma' khooy w booy elyoum
Of course I can come to the theater, and I want to sit together with you and with your sister
Akeed nebe enjee lil masraah ow nebe in ga'mez ma'ak wa ma'a okhtak.
I need to go down to see your new house
Aney lazem nenzil lota wa enshoof hoshak eljedeed /
Aney nabei nenzel lota nshof betak el ejdid
I can see the sky from the window
Aneey negdar enshoof elsamea mn el rowshen
I don't ever want to see you again
Aneey ma nebesh abadan nshofak marra Tanya

*In Libyan dialect, brother is *akh*, and dad is *booie*. However, "my dad" is *booy*, and "my brother" is *khoy*. "My sister" is *okhteh*, and "my mother" is *ommy*.

*With the knowledge you've gained so far, now try to create your own sentences!

To allow - Khali
To believe – Mesh tsadeg/nsadeg
Morning - Sabah
Except - Ma-a'ada
To promise - Mesh no3ed
Good night - Tisba le'khir
To recognize - Mesh na3reaf
People - Sh'khas
To move - Mesh net7aarek
Far - Ba3ed
Different – Mokhtalef
Man – Raajel
To enter – Mesh tokhosh/nkhosh
To receive – Mesh nastlem
Throughout - Khilal
Good afternoon - Masa le khir
Left / right - Yamen / yassaar (or) esaar
Him / her - Howe / Heya

I need to allow him to go with us, he is a different man now
Aney lazem enkhaleeh ejee maa;na howa rajel mokhtalef/tani tawa
I believe everything except this
Aney ennesadeg kol shay ma'ada haady
I promise to say good night to my parents each night
Aney noo3dek engool tesbah 'ala kheir la mowaleya kol Leila
The people from Jordan are very pleasant
El naas ili mn el ordon egnaynen halba
I need to find another hotel very quickly
Lazem nalgaa foondooq tany bsor'a
They need to receive a book for work
Homa mihtajin yestelmo el ketab lil elkhedma
I see the sun in the morning
Ane nnshoof el shams fel sobah
I am sorry, but he wants to follow her to the store
Aneey assef, laaken howa yebe yel7agha lel mahal
The house is on the right side of the street
El 7osh 'ala yemeen el shaaraa3

*For the possessive pronouns, her (*ha*) and him (*ah*), both become suffixes to the verb or noun. Concerning nouns: "her house" / *hosh'ha*, "his house" / *hosh'ah*, concerning cases regarding verbs, please see footnotes on page 19.

To wish - Mesh titmana
Bad – Ma'yanfaesh
To get - Mesh et-hasal
To forget - Mesh tansa
Everybody / everyone - Kolhom
Although - Maa' inna
To feel - Mesh et-hes
Great - 'Aadeem
Next - El jaye / janeb
To like - Mesh taajeabk
In front - Gedaam
Person - Shakhes
Behind - Ewara
Well - Kheer
Restaurant - Mat'em
Bathroom - Hemaam
Goodbye – Beslama

I don't want to wish you anything bad
Ane ma nebesh netmnalak haja ma'yanfaesh
I must forget everybody from my past to feel well
Lazem nansahom kolhom mesh nhess roo7ie bahie
I am next to the person behind you
Ane janb el shakhs ili warak
There is a great person in front of me
Fi shakhs 'adeem gedamy
I say goodbye to my friends
Ane bengool hawena la e-haaby aney benoda3 s'haaby
Where is the bathroom in the restaurant?
Ween el hamaam ili felmat'em?
She has to get a car before the next year
Heya lazem takhead syara abl el sana el jaye
I like the house, but it is very small
A3jabnie el7osh laken esghayeer halaba

*In Libyan Arabic there are two forms to define "next": *el jaye* or *janeb*. Janeb signifies "near" "close to" while el jaye signifies "the following," such as "the next year" / elsana el jaye.

To remove / to take out - Mesh etenhee
Please - Lawo samaht / ba'd ednek
Beautiful - Helo
To lift - Mesh tegaeem/tarfaa'
Include / including - Shamel / yeshmal
Belong - Melk
To hold - Yshed
To check - Net'akedo
Small - Esgheer
Real – Hoogani/7ug
Week - Esboo'
Size - Hajem
Even though - Maa' enna
Doesn't - (M)(F)(for adjectives) Mo / (for verbs) mish
So (as in then) - Yaani
So (as in very) - Halba
Price - Se'er

She wants to remove this door please
Hiyya tebe etna7y el bab hada law samaht
This doesn't belong here, I need to check again
Hada mesh mkannah ahney lazem netak'aed tani
This week the weather was very beautiful
el osboo' hada el jaw helwo halba
I need to know which is the real diamond
Ane mihtaaj ne'ref ama heya elma'saa elhoganeaa
We need to check the size of the house
Nehna nebo net'akedo mn hajem el 7osh
I want to lift this, so you need to hold it high
Nebee engeam hada fa enta lazem tshdaah foog
I can pay this although that the price is expensive
Ane negder nedfaa', maa'inna el see'r ghaaly halba
Including everything is this price correct?
Shameel kol shaae, elsee'r haad mazboot?

*Instead of saying "expensive," you sometimes use "too much" or "a lot." "A lot" means *halba*.

Other Useful Tools in Libyan Arabic

Countries of the Middle East
Bildein el-shar' el-awsatt
Lebanon - Lebnan
Syria - Suriyya
Jordan - L-ordon
Saudi Arabia - Es'oodya
Israel/Palestine/West Bank - Isra'eel/Falsteen/eldaffa el-gharbeyyeh
Bahrain - L-Bahrain
Yemen - L-Yamen
Oman - 'Oman
United Arab Emirates – L-Emarat
Kuwait - L-Kweit
Iraq - L-'Iraq
Qatar - Qitar
Morocco - El-Maghreb
Algeria - L-Jaza'ir
Libya - Leebya
Egypt - Maser
Tunisia – Tonis

Months
January - Shahr wahed
February - Shahr etneen
March - Shahr talata
April - Shahr arba'a
May - Shahr khamsa
June - Shahr seta
July - Shahr sab'a
August - Shahr tmanya
September - Shahr tes'a
October - Shahr 'ashra
November - Shahr ehdaash
December - Shahr etnaash

*Shahr literally means "month."

Days of the Week
Sunday - El ahed **Monday** - El etnyn **Tuesday** - Etlat **Wednesday** - El arrba3 **Thursday** - El khamees **Friday** - El jom'aa **Saturday** - El sabet

Seasons
Spring - El rebee' **Summer** - El seef **Autumn** - El khareef **Winter** - El shteeh

Cardinal Directions
North – Shaamaal
South – Jnoub
East – Sharag
West – Ghareb

Colors

Black - (M)Aswad (F)Sawda
White - (M)Abyad (F)Baida
Gray - (M)Rmahdeh (F) Rmahdiyyeh
Red - (M) Ahmar **(F)**Hamra
Blue - (M)Azra' (F)Zar'a
Yellow - (M) Asfar **(F)**Safra
Green - (M) Akhdar **(F)**Khadra
Orange - Berd'aneh
Purple - Ow rej wany
Brown - (M) Gahoey (F) gahoeaa

Numbers

One - Wahad
Two - Tnen
Three - Tlete
Four - Aarba'aa
Five - Khamsi
Six - Siti
Seven - Saba'aa
Eight - Tmene
Nine - Tisa'aa
Ten - A'ashra
Twenty - A'aishreen
Thirty - Tlateen
Forty - Arba'aeen
Fifty - Khamseen
Sixty - Sitteen
Seventy - Saba'aeen
Eighty - Tamaneen
Ninety - Tisi'in
Hundred - Miyi
Thousand - Alif
Million - Malyon

Conversational Arabic Quick and Easy

MOROCCAN DIALECT

YATIR NITZANY

THE MOROCCAN DIALECT

In Morocco, the most spoken language in daily life is Moroccan Darija or Moroccan Arabic, which is spoken by some 19 million people in the country. Modern Standard Arabic is used for official communications by the government and other public bodies but is not spoken socially. Moroccan Darija has a strong presence on television, social media, entertainment, cinema, and commercial advertising.

Darija is a language derived from a variety of Arabic dialects spoken in Morocco and belongs to the Maghrebi Arabic language continuum. It is mutually intelligible, to some extent, with Algerian Arabic and to a lesser extent with Tunisian Arabic. It shows a very strong historical and linguistic Berber, French, and Spanish influence.

Several of the Darija dialects belong to two genetically different groups: the pre-Hilalian and Hilalian dialects.

Pre-Hilalian dialects are a consequence of the early Arabization phases of the Maghreb, (which means West in Arabic and comprises much of the region of northern West Africa), from the 7th to the 12th centuries, concerning the main urban settlements, the harbors, the religious centers (zaouias), and the main trade routes.

Hilalian, or Bedouin, dialects were introduced to Morocco following the Hilalian Invasion. The origin of this language goes back to over 3000 years, being a singular evolution of the Punic language spoken by the Carthaginians under Amazigh influence. Moroccan Darija is characterized by a strong Amazigh stratum.

Spoken in: Morocco

ARABIC PRONUNCIATIONS

PLEASE MASTER THE FOLLOWING PAGE IN ARABIC PRONUNCIATIONS PRIOR TO STARTING THE PROGRAM

Kha. For Middle Eastern languages including Arabic, Hebrew, Farsi, Pashto, Urdu, Hindi, etc., and also German, to properly pronounce the kh or ch is essential, for example, *Khaled* (a Muslim name) or *Chanukah* (a Jewish holiday) or *Nacht* ("night" in German). The best way to describe kh or ch is to say "ka" or "ha" while at the same time putting your tongue at the back of your throat and blowing air. It's pronounced similarly to the sound that you make when clearing your throat. Please remember this whenever you come across any word containing a kh in this program.

Ghayin. The Arabic gh is equivalent to the "g" in English, but its pronunciation more closely resembles the French "r," rather than "g." Pronounce it at the back of your throat. The sound is equivalent to what you would make when gargling water. Gha is pronounced more as "rha," rather than as "ga." *Ghada* is pronounced as "rhada." In this program, the symbol for *ghayin* is gh, so keep your eyes peeled.

Aayin is pronounced as a'a, pronounced deep at the back of your throat. Rather similar to the sound one would make when gagging. In the program, the symbol for *aayin* is a'a, u'u, o'o, or i'i.

Ha is pronounced as "ha." Pronunciation takes place deep at the back of your throat, and for correct pronunciation, one must constrict the back of the throat and exhale air while simultaneously saying "ha." In the program, this strong h ("ha") is emphasized whenever *ha, ah, hi, he,* or *hu* is encountered.

NOTE TO THE READER

The purpose of this book is merely to enable you to communicate in the Moroccan Arabic dialect. In the program itself (pages 17-38) you may notice that the composition of some of those sentences might sound rather clumsy. This is intentional. These sentences were formulated in a specific way to serve two purposes: to facilitate the easy memorization of the vocabulary and to teach you how to combine the words in order to form your own sentences for quick and easy communication, rather than making complete literal sense in the English language. So keep in mind that this is not a phrase book!

As the title suggests, the sole purpose of this program is for conversational use only. It is based on the mirror translation technique. These sentences, as well as the translations are not incorrect, just a little clumsy. Latin languages, Semitic languages, and Anglo-Germanic languages, as well as a few others, are compatible with the mirror translation technique.

Many users say that this method surpasses any other known language learning technique that is currently out there on the market. Just stick with the program and you will achieve wonders!

Note to the Reader

Again, I wish to stress this program is by no means, shape, or form a phrase book! The sole purpose of this book is to give you a fundamental platform to enable you to connect certain words to become conversational. Please also read the "Introduction" and the "About Me" section prior to commencing the program.

In order to succeed with my method, please start on the very first page of the program and fully master one page at a time prior to proceeding to the next. Otherwise, you will overwhelm yourself and fail. Please do not skip pages, nor start from the middle of the book.

It is a myth that certain people are born with the talent to learn a language, and this book disproves that myth. With this method, anyone can learn a foreign language as long as he or she follows these explicit directions:

* Memorize the vocabulary on each page

* Follow that memorization by using a notecard to cover the words you have just memorized and test yourself.

* Then read the sentences following that are created from the vocabulary bank that you just mastered.

* Once fully memorized, give yourself the green light to proceed to the next page.

Again, if you proceed to the following page without mastering the previous, you are guaranteed to gain nothing from this book. If you follow the prescribed steps, you will realize just how effective and simplistic this method is.

The Program

Let's Begin! "Vocabulary" (Memorize the Vocabulary)

I | I am - Ana
With you – (Masc) Ana ma'ak / **(Masc/Fem)** Ana m'ak
With him / with her – (M) Ana m'ah / ana m'aha
With us - M'ana
For you - (M/F) Dyalk
Without him – Bla bih
Without them – Bla bihom
Always - Dima
Was – Kan
This, this is, it's – (M) Hada, had **(F)** hadi, had
Sometimes - Ba'ad lmarrat
Maybe – Yimken
You / you are / – (M) nta (F) nti
You (plural) - Ntouma
Are you?, is he?, is she? – Wash nta?/nti?, wash howa?, wash hiya?
Today – Lyom
Better – Hsan
He / he is - Huwa
She / she is – Hiya
From – Men

This is for you
(M) Hada dyalk (F) Hadi dyalk
I am from Morocco
Ana men lmaghrib
Are you from Casablanca?
Wash nta men Cazablanka?
I am with you
Ana m'ak
Sometimes you are with us at the mall
Ba'ad lmarrat nta m'ana f l mall
I am always with her
Ana dima m'aha
Are you without them today?
Wash nta/nti bla bihom lyom?
Sometimes I am with him
Ba'ad lmarrat ana m'ah

---

*In Arabic with the question "is it?", *wash* the "it" can pertain to either a masculine or feminine noun. However, whenever pertaining to a masculine or feminine noun, it will become *wash houwa* or *wash hiya*. For example, when referring to a feminine noun such as tonobil ("the car), "is it (the car in question) here?" / *Wash hiya hna?* When referring to a masculine noun such as *kelb* ("a dog), "is it (the dog in question) on the table?" *Wesh houwa foq tabla?* However, I yet again wish to stress that this isn't a grammar book!

I was - Kont
To be - **(M)** Ykun / **(F)** Tkun
The – El
Same – Bhal bhal / kif kif
Good - Mzyan
Here - Hna
Very - Bezaaf
And - W
Between - Bin
Now – Daba
Later / after / afterwards - Men ba'ad / ba'ad
If - Ila
Yes – Ah
To – L/tal
Tomorrow – Ghedda
You - **(M)** Nta / **(F)** nti
Also / too / as well – Tahuwwa (m) ta hiya (f)
With them – M'ahum

If it's between now and later
Ila bin daba o men ba'ad
It's better tomorrow
Ghedda hssen
This is good as well
Hadchi tahuwwa mezyan
To be the same person
Ykoun nefss shakhs
Yes, you are very good
Nta mezyan bzaf
I was here with them
Kent hna m'ahom
You and I
Nta w ana
The same day
Nefss nhar

Me – (read footnote)
Ok – Wakha
Even if - Hatta ila
No - La
Worse - Khayb ktar
Where - Fin
Everything - Kolshi
Somewhere – Shi blassa
What - Shno
Almost - Taqriban
There - (M) Kayn / (F) Kayna / tmma

Afterwards is worse
Men ba'ad khayeb ktar
Even if I go now
Hatta ila mchit daba
Where is everything?
Fein kolshi?
Maybe somewhere
Yemken chi blassa
What? I am almost there
Shnu ana taqriban temma
Where are you?
Finek
Where is the airport?
Fin ja lmatar?

*"There" has two meanings, so it is *kayna* or *tmma,* depending on the context. When we say "there is" we say *kayn* / but when we say "I am there" (place) we say *ana tmma*.

* *Fshi blassa* literally means "in a place."

*In Arabic, the pronoun "me" has several definitions. In relation to verbs, it's *liya*. *Liya* refers to any verb that relates to the action of doing something to someone or for someone.
For example, "tell me," "tell (to) me" / *(M) goul liya*.
'liya just means "me": "love me" / *ymoot 'liya*
Other variations (*ya*):
   * "on me" / *'liya*, "in me" / *fiya*
   * "to me" / *'liya*, "with me" / *maaya*

The same rule applies for "him" and "her"—both become suffixes: –*o* and –*a*. Basically all verbs pertinent to males end with *h*, and all pertinent to female end with ha.
   * "love her" / *kanebgheeha*
   * "love him" / *kanebgheeh*
   * "love them" / *kanebgheehom*
   * "love us" / *kanbghena*

Any verb that relates to doing someone to someone, for someone put *l*:
   * "tell her" / *goolliha*
   * "tell him" / *goollih*
   * "tell them" / *qoollihoum*
   * "tell us" / *goollina*

Adding you as a suffix in Arabic is *ak* or *lak*, female *ik* or *lik*.
   * "love you" / *kanebgheek (M+F)*
   * "tell you" / *qool-ek (M+F)*

House - Dar
In / at - Fe / be
Car – Tomobil
Already – Aslan
Good morning - sbah lkheir
How are you? – (M) Kidayr (F) Kidayra?
Where are you from? – **(M)** Mnein nta? **(F)** mnein nti?
Today - Lyom
Hello – Ahlan / Salam
What is your name? – **(M)** Chnu smitek (M+F)
How old are you? - Chehal f 'omrek? (M+F)
Son – Weld
Daughter - Bnt
To have – (M) 'Endo / (F) 'Endha
Doesn't - Ma… ash
Hard – S'eeb
Still – **(**M) Baqi / (F) baqa / (M+F) mazal
Then (or "so") – Men ba'ad/ ya'any / idan/ewa
In order to – Bash

She doesn't have a car, so maybe she is still at the house?
Ma'andhach tonobil idan tqdar tkun baqa f dar?
I am in the car already with your son and daughter
Ana aslan f tonobil maa weldek o bentek
Good morning, how are you today?
Ki dayer lyoum? Sbah lkhir
Hello, what is your name?
Ahlan/Salam, shenu smitak?
How old are you?
Sh-hal f 'omrak?
This is very hard, but it's not impossible
Hadchi s'eeb bzaf walakin mashi moustahil
Then where are you from?
Ewa mnin nta (M) Ewa mnin nti (F)

*In Arabic, possessive pronouns become suffixes to the noun. For example, in the translation for "your," *ak* is the masculine form, and *ik* is the feminine form.
- "your book" / Ktabek (M+F)
- "your house" / Darek (M+F)

*In Moroccan Arabic, *ka* is used to indicate cases of "to" or "to be able to." You will notice in the program that *ka* will quite often become a prefix to the verb "I want to learn," ana baghi net'allem or "to be able to go," *tkun qader tmchi*.

Thank you - Shukran
For - Dyal
Anything - Ay haja
That / That is – (F) Dik / (M) dak
Time - Mudda (duration)/ sa'a (if asking about the clock)
But - Walakin
No / not - Mashy / la'
I am not - Ana mashy
Away - Be'id
Late - M'atl
Similar – Bhal bhal
Another/ other – (M) akhor/lakhor (F) akhra/ lokhra
Side – Jnb
Until - Htta l
Yesterday – Lbareh
Without us – Bla bina
Since – Mlli
Day - Youm
Before – Qbel

Thanks for everything
Shukran 'ela kolshi
It's almost time
hada teqriban lweqt
I am not here, I am away
Ana mashy hena, ana b'id
That is a similar house
Had dar bhalha
I am from the other side
Ana men jiha lokhra
But I was here until late yesterday
Walakin kent m'atel lbareh
I am not at the other house
Ana mashy fi dar lokhra

*In Moroccan Arabic, with negations such as "no," "not," "doesn't," "can't," and "don't," use either *mashy* or *la*. *La* is used to indicate cases such as "are you here" – *nta hena* – and you then reply "no," *la*. *Mashy* is used to indicate cases of "not," "doesn't," or "don't," for example: "I am not at the other house" is *ana machy f dar lokhra*. In some instances both cases of *la* and *mashy* may be used, for example; "can you come?" "No, I can't," *la*.

* In Moroccan Arabic, in the event that "doesn't" is used regarding negations of verbs, the following requirements must precede and follow *ma ... ch/sh*, for example: "she doesn't have the beer" (The verb "have" is *aand*) – *heya ma'andhach elbeera*.

*In Moroccan Darija Arabic, there are three definitions for time:
* "time" / *mudda* refers to "era", "moment period," "duration of time."
* "time(s)" / *marra(t)* / *khatra(t)* refers to "occasion" or "frequency."
* "time" / *sa'a* references "hour," "what time is it?"

What time is it? - Chehal sa'a
I say / I am saying – Kangoul
I want Ana bghet/ bghet
Without you –Bla bik
Everywhere /wherever – F ay blassa
I go - Ka nemshy
With - Ma'
My – Dyalli
Cousin (paternal) - (M) Wld 'amy / (F) bnt 'amy / (P) (M) wlaad 'amy / (P)(F) banaat 'amy
Cousin (maternal) - (M) Wld khaly / (F) bnt khali / (P)(M) wlaad khaly / (P)(F) bnat khaly
I need - Khasny
Right now – Daba
Night – Lil
To see - Nshoof
Light – Ddo
Outside – Barra / 'ala barra
Without – Bla
Happy - Farhan
I see / I am seeing - Nshoof

I am saying no / I say no
Nqool la'
I want to see this today
Bghit nchouf hadchi lyoum
I am with you everywhere
Ana maak fin ma kan
I am happy without my cousins here
Ana Farhan bla wlad 'ammi hna
I need to be there at night
Khassni nkoun temma b lil
I see light outside
Kanchouf ddo 'ela barra
What time is it right now?
Shehal f sa'a daba?

*"Mine" / *dyali* is also a possessive pronoun. *Dyali* means "my" but also becomes a suffix to a noun. Nouns ending in a vowel end with *–teh*. Nouns ending with a consonant end with *–eh*. For example:
  * "cousin" / *wld el 'amm*, "my cousin" / *wld 'ammy*
  * "cup" / *kass*, "my cup" / *kassi*

For second and third person masculine noun, *ibin* ("son"), male (S) *ak*, (P) *kom*) and female (S) *ik*, (P) *kum*). "His" – *Ilo* / "hers" – *ila*, noun endings will be *o* (for male) and *a* (for female).
  * "your son" / *weldek*, "your (plural) son" / *weldkoum*
  * "his son" / *weldou*, "her son" / *weldha*
  * "our son" / *weldna*, "their son" *weldhoum*

For second and third person feminine noun: "car" / *tonobil*
  * "your car" / *tonobiltek*, "your (plural) car" / *tonobiltkoum*
  * "his car" / *tonobilto*, "her car" / *tonobiltha*
  * "our car" / *tonobiltna*, "their car" / *tonobilthoum*

*****This *isn't* a phrase book! The purpose of this book is *solely* to provide you with the tools to create *your own* sentences!**

Place – Blasa
Easy – Sahel
To find - Telqa
To look for / to search – Qalleb 'ela
Near / Close – Qreb
To wait – Tsenna
To sell - (M) Ybee' / (F) tbee'
To use - Sta'mel
To know - T'aref
To decide – Qarrer
Between - Bin
Both – Bjouj / jouj
To – La (to indicate a noun), ka/kan (to indicate a verb)

This place it's easy to find
Had lblassa sahla telqa
I want to look for this next to the car
Bghit nqalleb 'ela hadshi hda tonobil
I am saying to wait until tomorrow
Kangol lik tsenna tal ghedda
This table is easy to sell
Had tabla sahel tba'
I want to use this
Bghit neste'mel hadshi
I need to know where is the house
Khassni ne'raf dar fin
I want to decide between both places
Bghit nkhtar bin jouj blayss

*In Moroccan Arabic, in the event that "doesn't" is used regarding negations of verbs, the following requirements must precede and follow ma … ch/sh, for example: "she doesn't have the beer" (The verb "have" is *aand*) – *heya ma'andhach elbeera*.

*In Moroccan Arabic, to indicate "to," either *l* or *ka/kan* may be used. *L* is placed preceding a noun. In a phrase such as "going to a place," for instance, *ka/kan* is used to precede a verb, or to indicate "in order to." In certain instances, both *ka/kan* and *l* may be used, for example: "in order to go to Casablanca," *bach nemchi l Casablanca*.

Because - Heet
To buy – Shry
They - Huma
Them | their – Huma
Bottle - Qar'a
Book – Ktab
Mine - Dyali
To understand – Tefhem
Problem - Mushkil
I do / I am doing - N'mel / kandir
Of - De
To look – Shoof
Myself – Rassi
Enough – Kaafi
Food / water - Makla / ma
Each/ every/ entire/ all – Koll
Hotel - Otel

I like this hotel because I want to look at the beach
'Jebni had l otel heet bghit nshuf l bhar
I want to buy a bottle of water
Bghit neshri qar'a del ma
I do this every day
Kandir hadshi kol nhar
Both of them have enough food
Bjujhum 'andhum lmakla kafya
That is the book, and that book is mine
Hada huwa lktab, o had lktab dyali
I need to understand the problem
Khassni nfhem lmushkil
I see the view of the city from the hotel
Kanchof lmandar dyal lmdina mn l otel
I do my homework today
Kandir wajibati lmanziliya kol nhar
My entire life (*all my life*)
Hyati kamla

*"Both of them" is *bjojhum*

I like - Kay'jebny
There is / There are – Kayen
Family / Parents - 'Aila / walidin
Why – 'Alash
To say – Goul
Something - She haja
To go – Nmshy / (M) yimshy / (F) timshy
Ready – Wajed
Soon – Qreb
To work – Nkhdem / (M) yikhdem / (F) tikhdim
Who – Shkoun
To know - 'Aref
That (conjunction) – Belli, wash

I like to be at my house with my parents
kay'jbni nkoun f dar m'aa walidiya
I want to know why I need to say something important
bghit ne'raf 'elash khassni ngoul chi haja mouhimma
I am there with him
Ana temma m'ah
I am busy, but I need to be ready soon
Ana mechghoul walakin khassni nkoun wajed qreb
I like to go to work
Kay'jebni nemshi nekhdem
Who is there?
Shkoun tmma?
I want to know if they are here, because I want to go outside
Bghit ne'raf wash houma hna hit baghi nkhrej 'ela berra
There are seven dolls
Kaynin seb'a dyal lmounikat
I need to know that it is a good idea
Khassni ne'raf wash hadi fikra mzyana

*In the last sentence, we use "that" as a conjunction (*wash*) and a demonstrative pronoun *(M) hada / (F) hadik)*.

How much / how many – Besh-hal
To bring – Jib
With me – M'aya
Instead – Blast
Only – Gheir / ghi
When – Fuqash / imta
Or – Aw
I can / Can I – Nqdar / yimken leya
Were - Kano
Without me – Bla biya
Fast - Deghya
Slow – Bchwiya
Cold – Bared
Inside – L'dakhel
To eat – Kla
Hot – Skhoon
To Drive – Tsog

How much money do I need to bring with me?
Chehal dyal lflouss khassni njib ma'ya
Instead of this cake, I want that cake
F blast had lkika bghit had lkika
Only when you can
Ghi fash tqdar
They were without me yesterday
kanou bla biya lbareh
Do I need to drive the car fast or slow?
Khasni nsog tonobil b zerba wla bchwiya
It is cold inside the library
kayn lberd ldakhel fel mektaba
Yes, I like to eat this hot for my lunch
ah, kay'ejbeni nakol skhon fel ghda
I can work today
Neqdar nkhdem lyoum

*"Were" is *ykun*, but for "they were," is *kanu* "We were" is *konna*.

*"I can" and "can I?" is *yimkn lya*. "You can" or "can you?" is *yimkin leek?*

To answer – Redd / jaweb
To fly - Teer
Time / Times - Mrra / Mrrat
To travel – Safer
To learn - Net'allam / (M) yt'alam / (F) tet'alam
How – Kifash
To swim - N'oom / (M) y'oom / (F) t'oom
To practice – Ytrina
To play - L'aab
To leave – Tkhelli
Many /much /a lot - Kteer, bezaaf
I go to - Kanemshy
First - Luwl
World – 'Aalamm

I want to answer many questions
Bghit njawb bzaf dyal as'ila
I must fly to Dubai today
Ana khasny teer l Dubai lyom
I need to learn how to swim at the pool
Ana khassni net'allam n'oum fla pissine
I want to learn to play better tennis
Ana bghit nt'allem nl'ab hssen f tennis
I want to leave this here for you when I go to travel the world
Bghit nkhelli hadshi hna 'ela qblek fash nmchi nsafer f l'alam
Since the first time
Men lmerra lowla
The children are yours
Lwlad dyalek

*In Moroccan Darija Arabic, "to leave (something)" is *tkheli*. "To leave (a place)" is *tkhrej*.

- In Moroccan Darija Arabic, there are three definitions for time:
- "time" / *mudda* refers to "era", "moment period," "duration of time."
- "time(s)" / *marra(t)* /*khatra(t)* refers to "occasion" or "frequency."
- "time" / *sa'a* references "hour," "what time is it?"

*With the knowledge you've gained so far, now try to create your own sentences!

Nobody / anyone – Ta wahed
Against - Dedd
Us – Hna
To visit - Yzoor
Mom / Mother – Oumm/mmi
To give – 'Aty
Which - Eshmen
To meet - Tlaqa
Someone – She wahed
Just - Gheir
To walk - Tmasha
Around – Hawl
Towards - Tijah
Than - Min
Nothing – Walu / hata haja / hata shi

Something is better than nothing
Shi haja hsan min walu
I am against him
Ana deddo
Is there anyone here?
Kayn shi hed hna
We go to visit my family each week
Kanmchiw bash nzoro l'a'ila kul simana
I need to give you something
Ana khasny a'tyk shi haja
Do you want to go meet someone?
Baghi temshi tlaqa chi wahed
I was here on Wednesdays as well
Hta larb'a kent hna
Do you do this every
Nta katdir hadshi kulla nhar
You need to walk around, but not towards the house
Khassek tmshi hawl, mashi f ttijah dar

---

*In Arabic, when using the pronoun "you" as a direct and indirect object pronoun (the person who is actually affected by the action that is being carried out) in relation to a verb, the pronoun "you" becomes a suffix to that verb. That suffix becomes *ak* (masc.) *ik* (fem.).

* "to give" / *a'teh*: "to give you" / *a'teek*
* "to tell" / *qool*: "to tell you" / *qoolak* (m.), *qoolik* (f.)
* "see you" / *nshoofak*: "to see you" (plural) / *nshoofkom (m+f)*

For third person male, add *o* and *on* for plural, for female add *a* and *on* for plural.

* "tell him" / *goolih*
* "tell her" / *gooliha*
* "see them" / *nshoofhom*
* "see us " / *shoofna*

I have – 'Andy
Don't – Maddirch
Friend - Saheb
To borrow – Tsellef
To look like / resemble – Tban bhal
Like (preposition) – Bhal
Grandfather – Jidd
To want – Tebghi
To stay – Bqa
To continue - Stamer
Way – Treq
I don't - Makandirch
To show - Wary
To prepare – Tsayb
I am not going - Maghadish

Do you want to look like Salim
bghiti tban bhal salim
I want to borrow this book for my grandfather
bghit ntsellef had lktab mn 'and jeddi
I want to drive and to continue on this way to my house
bghit nsog o nkemmel f had treq tal dar
I have a friend there, that's why I want to stay in Marrakesh
andi sahbi temma, dakshi 'elash baghi nebqa f marrakch
I am not going to see anyone here
maghadi nchuf ta wahed hna
I need to show you how to prepare breakfast
khassni nwerrik kifash tsayb lftor
Why don't you have the book?
'elash ma'andeksh lktab?
That is incorrect, I don't need the car today
hadshi mashi sheh, mamehtajch tonobil lyoum

*In Moroccan Arabic the case of "you don't have" is *ma'andkch*.

To remember - 'Aql 'ala
Your - Ta'ek/dialek (M+F)
Number - Raqm
Hour - Sa'aa
Dark / darkness – Mdallem/dlam
About / on the - 'Ala
Grandmother - Jedda / my grandmother – Jeddaty
Five - Khamsa
Minute / minutes - Dqeeqa / dqayq
More – Ktar
To think – Fakker
To do – Deer
To come – Ajy
To hear - Sma'
Last – Akher

You need to remember my number
Nte khasak t'aql 'ala raqmy
This is the last hour of darkness
Hady akher sa'aa dial dlam
I want to come and to hear my grandmother speak Arabic
Bghit nji o nsme' jedda kathdar bel 'arbiya
I need to think more about this, and what to do
Khassni nfekker kter f hadshi, o chnu yddar
From here to there, it's only five minutes
Men hna l lheh, ghi khamssa dqayq
The school on the mountain
L madrasa f jbel

*In Moroccan Arabic *dial* means "for (someone)" or "for" (something)".

To leave - Nkhroj
Again - T'awed
Morocco - Lmaghrib
To take - Nakhod
To try - Jreb
To rent – Kra
Without her - Bla biha
We are – Hna
To turn off - Tfa
To ask – Suwal
To stop - Wqf
Permission - Edn

He needs to leave and rent a house at the beach
Khassou ymchi w ykri dar fel bhar
I want to take the test without her
Bghit ndowez lemtihan bla biha
We are here a long time
Hna hna mudda twela
I need to turn off the lights early tonight
Khasni ntfi dwaw bekri lyoum
We want to stop here
Bghina nhebssou hna
We are from Rabbat
Hna men rbat
The same building
Nefss l'imara
I want to ask permission to leave
Bghi ntleb l idn bash nmchi
I want to sleep
Bghit n'as

*Morocco is officially referred to as *al-mamleka al-maghrabiya* (literal meaning: "The Kingdom of Morocco").

To open – Ftah / yhell
A bit, a little, a little bit – Shwiya
To pay – Nkhales
Once again - Merra khra
There isn't/ there aren't – Makayn
Sister - Okht
To hope - Tmna
To live - 'Esh
Nice to meet you - Metsharfin
Name - Smya
Last name - Kniyya
To return – Rja'
Door - Baab

I need to open the door for my sister
Khasny nhell lbab l khty
I need to buy something
Khasny nshry she haja
I want to meet your sisters
Khasny netlaqa khwatatek
Nice to meet you, what is your name and your last name
Metsharfin, shenu smitak w knitek?
To hope for a little better
Tmna shwya hsan
I want to return from the United States and to live in Qatar without problems
Bghit nerje' men lmirikan o n'ish f Qatar bla mashakil
Why are you sad right now?
'Alash mqllaq deba?
There aren't any people here
Makaynch nass hna
There isn't enough time to go to Agadir today
Makaynsh lweqt lkafi bash tmshi l Agadir lyum

*In Moroccan Darija Arabic, regarding the verb "to meet," there are two separate cases to define this verb: *tjtame'*and *tlaqa*, depending of the context. To meet for business is *tjtame'*. To meet for getting acquainted is *tlaqa*. In the sentence, "Do you want to go meet someone?" (the sister, getting acquainted with her), it's *tlaqa*.

*This *isn't* a phrase book! The purpose of this book is *solely* to provide you with the tools to create *your own* sentences!

To happen – Wqa'
To order – T'amer
To drink – Shrob
Excuse me - (M) Smah le / (F) semhi le
Child - (**M**) Weld, (**F**) Bint
Woman - Mra
To begin / to start - Bda
To finish - Saala
To help - 'Awen
To smoke - Kma
To love - Bgha / moot 'ala
To talk / to speak – Tkallam/ hdar

This must happen today
Hadshi khaso ywqa' l-yom
Excuse me, my child is here as well
Smah le, weldi hena tahuwwa
I love you
Kanbghek/kanmoot 'alik
I see you
Kanshufek
I need you at my side
Mehtajek jenbi
I need to begin soon to be able to finish at 3 o'clock in the afternoon
Khasny nebda bekri bash nkun qader nsali m'a tlata dyal le'chiya
I need help
Ana khasny 'awn
I don't want to smoke once again
Mabaghich nkmi merra khra
I want to learn how to speak Arabic
Bghit nt'allem kifash nhdar bel 'arbiya

*"To be able to" is *ka+verb*. For example, "To be able to learn" (learn is *net'allam*) – *ka net'allam*.

 *In Moroccan Arabic to signify "love" we can either use *moot 'ala* or *kanbghi*.

To read - Neqra
To write – Nekteb
To teach - T'allem
To close – Qfal / sedd
To choose - Khtar
To prefer - Tfaddel
To put - Hott
Less - Qal
Sun - Chemch
Month – Shhar
I talk – Tkalm / hdar
Exact – Bddabt

I need this book to learn how to read and write in Arabic because I want to teach in Egypt
Khasny had lektab bash nt'allem kifash neqra o nekteb bel 'arbiya hit bghit nqarri f misr
I want to close the door of the house
Bghit nsedd lbab dyal dar
I prefer to put the gift here
Kan-faddill hott el cadeaux hena
I want to pay less than you for the dinner
Bghit nkhalles qall mennek ela l'cha
I speak with the boy and the girl in French
Kanhdar m'a lweld o lbent bel fransawiya
There is sun outside today
Kayna chemch ela berra lyoum
Is it possible to know the exact date?
Momkin ne'raf tarikh bddabt?

* "For the" is *lel*
* "In" is *fel*
* **With the knowledge you've gained so far, now try to create your own sentences!**

To exchange (money) – Tsarraf
To call – N'ayet
Brother – Akh
Dad – 'Ab
To sit - Gles
Together – Ma'a
To change – Tghayyer / tbaddel
Of course - Tab'an
Welcome – Merhba
During - Khelal
Years - **(S)**'Aam/ **(P)** 'a'waam
Sky – Sema
Up – Foq
Down - Taht
Sorry – Smeh li
To follow - Tbaa'
To the - Le
Big - Kbir
New - Jdid
Never / ever - 'Omry ma
Him / Her - O / a *(read footnote)*

I don't want to exchange this money at the bank
Mabghitch nsarref had lflouss fel banka
I call my brother and my dad today
N'ayyet ela khoya o baba lyoum
Of course I can come to the theater, and I want to sit together with you and with your sister
Tb'an nqdar nji l massrah, w bghit ngles ma'ak nta w khtak
I need to go down to see your new house
Khasny nhbet lteht bash nshuf darek jdida
I can see the sky from the window
Nqdar nshuf sema men charjem
I am sorry, but he wants to follow her to the store
Smeh li, walakin baghi yetb'ha l lmahal
I don't want to see you again
Mabqitch baghi nshufek merra khra

*In Moroccan Darija dialect, brother is *akh,* and dad is *ab.* However, "my dad" is *baba/lwalid* and "my brother" is *khooya.* "My sister" is *khtey,* and "my mother" is *mama/lwalida.* For the possessive pronouns, her (h*a*) and him (*o*), both become suffixes to the verb or noun. Concerning nouns: her house / *darha,* his house / *daro.* Concerning cases regarding verbs, please see page 19.

To allow - Smah
To believe – 'Aamen
Morning – Sbaah
Except - Ma 'ada
To promise - Waa'ed
Good night - Layla sa'eeda
To recognize - T'araf
People - Naas
To move - Harrak
Far - B'eed
Different – Mekhtalef
Man – Rajel
To enter - Dkhal
To receive – Twssl b
Throughout - Khilal
Good evening – Mselkhir
Left / right - Lisar/limen

I need to allow him to go with us, he is a different man now
Ana khasny smah lo ymshy ma'na, huwa rajil mekhtlef deba
I believe everything except this
Ana m'amen b koll-shi ma 'ada hadshi
I promise to say good night to my parents each night
Ana wa'edt ngoul lwalidiya Leila sa'ida kul lila
The people from Jordan are very pleasant
Nass fel ordon driyfin bzaf
I need to find another hotel very quickly
Khasny nelqa otel akhor dghya
They need to receive a book for work
Khasshum ytwesslo b ktab ela qbel lkhedma
I see the sun in the morning
Kanshuf chemch f sbah
The house is on the right side of the street
Dar f limen dyal zenqa

To wish - Tmanna
Bad - Khayeb
To get - Yakhod
To forget - Nsa
Everybody / Everyone - Kolshi/koll wahed
Although - Wakha
To feel – Hess
Great – Mohim
Next (as in close, near) - Hda
Next (as in next year) - Jai
To like – Bgha
In front – Qoddam
Person - Shakhs
Behind - Mowra
Well – Hssen
Restaurant - Restora
Bathroom - Beit el maa / twalet
Goodbye - Besalama

I don't want to wish you anything bad
Mabghitch netmenna lik chi haja khayba
I must forget everybody from my past to feel well
Khasny nsa kulshi mn lmadi bash nhess hsen
I am next to the person behind you
Ana hda chakhs li mowrak
There is a great person in front of me
Kayn chakhss mouhimm qoddami
I say goodbye to my friends
Kangoul bslama l shabi
Where is the bathroom in the restaurant?
Fein twalet f restoraa?
She has to get a car before the next year
Khassha tchri tonobil qbel l'am jay
I like the house, but it is very small
'Ajbani dar, walakin sghera bzaf

**Hda* literally means "side." In Arabic, it refers to "next." *Hdaya* is "besides me" and *hdak* is "besides you."

To remove / to take out - Hayd / zuwl
Please - 'Afaak
Beautiful - (**M**)Zwin, (**F**)Zwina
To lift – Hzz
Include / Including – Shmel
Belong – Ntami
To hold - Shedd
To check – Shoof
Small - Sgheer
Real - Haqeeqy
Week - Simana
Size – Qyass
Even though - Wkha
Doesn't - Mashy
So (as in "then") **–** Ya'ny
So (as in "very") **-** Bezaaf
Price – Taman

She wants to remove this door please
Bagha thayyed had lbab 'afak
This doesn't belong here, I need to check again
Hadshi makayntamish l hna, khasny nshuf 'awttani
This week the weather was very beautiful
Had simana ljaw kan zwin bzaf
I need to know which is the real diamond
Khasny ne'raf finahiya diamond l-hqeeqya
We need to check the size of the house
Khasna nshufu qyass dyal ddar
I want to lift this, so you need to hold it high
Khassni nhezz hadi ya'ni khassek thezha lfoq
I can pay this even though that the price is expensive
Nqdar nkhalless hadshi wakha taman ghali
Including everything is this price correct?
Shmel kulshi, wash taman sheh?

Countries of the Middle East
Bouldan sharq l awsat
Lebanon - Lobnan
Syria – Sourya
Jordan – L'ordon
Saudi Arabia – Sa'oudiya
Israel /Palestine /West Bank - Isra'eel / filisteen/ diffa algharbiyya
Bahrain – L'bahrein
Yemen – L'yaman
Oman - 'Oman
United Arab Emirates – L'emarat al'arabya el-motaheda
Kuwait – Lkouwet
Iraq – L'iraq
Qatar - Qatar
Morocco - Lmaghrib
Algeria – L'jazayer
Libya - Leebya
Egypt –Missra
Tunisia – Tunes

Months

Months

January – Janvye
February – Fevrye
March – Mars
April – Avril
May - May
June – Jwin
July – Jwiye
August – Out
September – Semptembre
October - Oktobar
November – Novembre
December – Decembre

Days of the Week
Sunday - Lhadd
Monday - Tnin
Tuesday - Tlat
Wednesday - Larb'a
Thursday - Lkhmiss
Friday - Jem'a
Saturday – Sabt

Seasons

Spring – Rbee'
Summer - Seif
Autumn – Khreef
Winter - Shetta

Cardinal Directions

North - Shamaal
South - Janoob
East – Sharq
West - Gharb

Colors

Black - Khal
White - Byad
Gray – Gri
Red – Hmar
Blue - Zreq
Yellow - Sfar
Green - Khdar
Orange – Lemoony
Purple - Mov
Brown - Qahwi

Numbers

One - Wahed
Two - Juj
Three – Tlata
Four - Rb'aa
Five - Khamsa
Six – Stta
Seven - Sab'aa
Eight - Tmenya
Nine - Ts'oud
Ten - 'Ashra
Twenty - 'Eshreen
Thirty - Tlaten
Hundred – Mya
Thousand – Alf
Million – Mlyoun

Conversational
Arabic
Quick and Easy

TUNISIAN ARABIC

YATIR NITZANY

TUNISIAN ARABIC DIALECT

Tunisia is a North African country bordering the Mediterranean Sea and Sahara Desert, and has an estimated 11.4 million inhabitants.

In Tunisia, a set of dialects of Maghrebi Arabic are spoken by eleven million speakers and are referred to as Tounsi, Tunisian or Derja that means "everyday language." This distinguishes the languages from the official Modern Standard Arabic (MSA).

Like other Maghrebi dialects, its vocabulary is mostly Arabic but with significant Berber and Latin inclusions. Tunisian merges into Algerian Arabic and Libyan Arabic at the borders of the country.
Tunisian Arabic is mostly intelligible to speakers of other Maghrebi dialects but is hard to understand or is unintelligible for speakers of Middle Eastern Arabic. Its pronunciation, vocabulary and syntax are different enough from MSA and Classical Arabic to not be mutually intelligible with either of them. It also has many loanwords from French, Turkish, Italian, and Spanish.

There is much multilingualism within Tunisia, and Tunisians often mix Tunisian with French, English, Standard Arabic, or other languages in daily speech. There has been integration of new French and English words with Tunisian Arabic, notably in technical fields, or replacement of old French and Italian loan words with standard Arabic ones.

Tunisian Arabic is also closely related to Maltese, which is a separate language that descended from Tunisian and Siculo-Arabic.

Spoken in: Tunisia

ARABIC PRONUNCIATIONS

PLEASE MASTER THE FOLLOWING PAGE IN ARABIC PRONUNCIATIONS PRIOR TO STARTING THE PROGRAM

Kha. For Middle Eastern languages including Arabic, Hebrew, Farsi, Pashto, Urdu, Hindi, etc., and also German, to properly pronounce the kh or ch is essential, for example, *Khaled* (a Muslim name) or *Chanukah* (a Jewish holiday) or *Nacht* ("night" in German). The best way to describe kh or ch is to say "ka" or "ha" while at the same time putting your tongue at the back of your throat and blowing air. It's pronounced similarly to the sound that you make when clearing your throat. Please remember this whenever you come across any word containing a kh in this program.

Ghayin. The Arabic *gh* is equivalent to the "g" in English, but its pronunciation more closely resembles the French "r," rather than "g." Pronounce it at the back of your throat. The sound is equivalent to what you would make when gargling water. Gha is pronounced more as "rha," rather than as "ga." *Ghada* is pronounced as "rhada." In this program, the symbol for ghayin is gh, so keep your eyes peeled.

Aayin is pronounced as *a'a*, pronounced deep at the back of your throat. Rather similar to the sound one would make when gagging. In the program, the symbol for *aayin* is a'a, u'u, o'o, or i'i.

Ha is pronounced as "ha." Pronunciation takes place deep at the back of your throat, and for correct pronunciation, one must constrict the back of the throat and exhale air while simultaneously saying "ha." In the program, this strong h ("ha") is emphasized whenever *ha, ah, hi, he,* or *hu* is encountered.

NOTE TO THE READER

The purpose of this book is merely to enable you to communicate in Tunisian Arabic. In the program itself (pages 17-38) you may notice that the composition of some of those sentences might sound rather clumsy. This is intentional. These sentences were formulated in a specific way to serve two purposes: to facilitate the easy memorization of the vocabulary and to teach you how to combine the words in order to form your own sentences for quick and easy communication, rather than making complete literal sense in the English language. So keep in mind that this is not a phrase book!

As the title suggests, the sole purpose of this program is for conversational use only. It is based on the mirror translation technique. These sentences, as well as the translations are not incorrect, just a little clumsy. Latin languages, Semitic languages, and Anglo-Germanic languages, as well as a few others, are compatible with the mirror translation technique.

Many users say that this method surpasses any other known language learning technique that is currently out there on the market. Just stick with the program and you will achieve wonders!

Note to the Reader

Again, I wish to stress this program is by no means, shape, or form a phrase book! The sole purpose of this book is to give you a fundamental platform to enable you to connect certain words to become conversational. Please also read the "Introduction" and the "About Me" section prior to commencing the program.

In order to succeed with my method, please start on the very first page of the program and fully master one page at a time prior to proceeding to the next. Otherwise, you will overwhelm yourself and fail. Please do not skip pages, nor start from the middle of the book.

It is a myth that certain people are born with the talent to learn a language, and this book disproves that myth. With this method, anyone can learn a foreign language as long as he or she follows these explicit directions:

* Memorize the vocabulary on each page

* Follow that memorization by using a notecard to cover the words you have just memorized and test yourself.

* Then read the sentences following that are created from the vocabulary bank that you just mastered.

* Once fully memorized, give yourself the green light to proceed to the next page.

Again, if you proceed to the following page without mastering the previous, you are guaranteed to gain nothing from this book. If you follow the prescribed steps, you will realize just how effective and simplistic this method is.

THE PROGRAM

Let's Begin! "Vocabulary" (Memorize the Vocabulary)

I	I am	Ena
	With you	(Male/Female) M'aak
	With him / with her	M'aah / m'aaha
	With us	M'aana
	For you	(M/F) Lik *(read the footnote below)*
	Without him	Min ghiru (or 'blesh bih')
	Without them	Min ghirhom (or 'blesh bihom')
	Always	Dima
	Was	Ken
	This, this is, it's	(M) Hedha / (F) Hedhi
	Today	Lyoom
	Sometimes	Se'aat
	Maybe	Yomkon
	You, you are, are you?	(M)/(F)Inti
	Better	Ahsen / khir / ahla
	You (plural)	(M)/(F) Entom
	He, he is	Howa
	She, she is	Hiya
	From	Min

Sentences from the vocabulary (now you can speak the sentences and connect the words)

This is for you
Hedha/Hedhi lik

I am from Tunisia
Ena min Tunes

Are you from Tunisia?
Enti min Tunes?

I am with you
Ena m'aak

Sometimes you are with us at the mall
Se'aat enti m'aana fil mall

I am always with her
Ena dima m'aaha

Are you without them today?
Inti min ghirhom lyoom?

Sometimes I am with him
Ena se'aat m'aah

*In Tunisian Arabic, there are gender rules. As of the second pronoun "you", saying for example "for you", it is the same regardless of the gender Lik. However, when referring to the third person, gender distinction comes into play, in which case "for him" translates to Lih and "for her" translates to "liha". However, if the sentence was "I did it for you" (i.e., I did this only because you are a special friend to me or because you mean a lot to me), here in this context we use ala khatrek either for a girl or a boy.

I was	Ena kont
To be	(M) Ykoon / (F) tkoon
The	El, l
Same / like *(as in similar)*	Nafs / kif
Good	(M) Behi / (F) Behya
Here	Hooni
Very	Barsha / yecer
And	W'
Between	Ma bin / bin
Now	Taw, tawa
Later / After / afterwards	Baa'diin / baa'd
If	I'tha / law
Yes	Ayh
To	L'
Tomorrow	Ghodwa
Person	Shakhs
Also / too / as well	Zeda / hatta *(read footnote)*

If it's between now and later
I'tha kein bin tawa w' baa'd
It's better tomorrow
Ghodwa khir / ahsen
This is good as well
(M) Hedha behi zeda (F) Hedhi behya zeda
To be the same person
(M) Ykoun nafs el shakhs / (F) tkoun nafs el shakhs
Yes, you are very good
(M) Ayh, inti behi barsha / (F) ayh, inti behya barsha
I was here with them
Ena kont hooni m'aahom
You and I
Inti w'ena
The same day
Nafs el-yoom

*In the Arabic language, adjectives usually proceed the noun. For example, "the same day" is *nafs el yom*. For example: "small house" / *dar sgheera*, "tall person" / *shakhs tweel*, "short person" / *shakhs k'seer*.
There are exceptions, though. For example, when expressing admiration or something impressive, we can say, "How big is this house?" / *Ma akbarha hal dar?*
*In Tunisian Arabic there are two forms to signify "if" / *idha* and *law*. "If it's raining tomorrow, I am not going," for instance, in this case, we use "*idha*." For "if I knew that this will happen, I wouldn't go to visit her," here the "if" is like "had I" and law will be used.
*In the Tunisian dialect, to express "too/also/as well" you use *hatta* at the beginning of the sentence. For example, "I love you too" / *Hatta ena nhebek*. You use *zeda* at the end of the sentence. "I love you too" / *Ena nhebek zeda*.
Behi in the Tunisian dialect has two connotations: 1) "Okay" / "I agree"; and 2) "Good" / "nice."

The Program

Me	Ni / li *(read footnote)*
Ok	Ayh/ ok / beh/ behi
Even if	Hatta law
No	La
Worse	Akhyeb
Where	Ween
Everything	Kol shay
Somewhere	Fi blasa ma
What	Shnou / shnowa
Almost	Takriban
There	Ghadi
I go	Nemshi

Afterwards is worse
Baa'diin akhyeb
Even if I go now
Hatta I'dha mshit taw
Where is everything?
Ween kol shay?
Maybe somewhere
Yomkon fi blasa ma
What? I am almost there
Shnou? ena takriban ghadi
Where are you?
Enti ween?

*In Arabic, the pronoun "me" has several definitions. In relation to verbs, it's *ni* or *li*. *Li* refers to any verb that relates to the action of doing something to someone, or for someone.
For example, "tell me," "tell (to) me" / (M/F) *kolli*.
Ni just means "me": "love me" / *heb'ni* or "see me" / *shoof'ni*
Other variations ([y]ya, i): on me" / *'aliyya*, "in me" / *fiyya*, "to me" / *liyya*, "with me" / *m'aaya*, "in front of me" / *koddemi*, "from me" / *minni*
The same rule applies for "him" and "her"—both become suffixes: –*o* and –*a*. Basically all verbs pertinent to males end with *o*, and all pertinent to female end with *a*.
"love her" / *nhebha*, "love him" / *nhebbu*, "love them" / *nhebhom*, "love us" / *nhebna*
Any verb that relates to doing something to someone, or for someone put l:
"tell her" / *kolha*, "tell him" / *kollu*, "tell them" / *kolhom*, "tell us" / *kolna*
Adding you as a suffix in Arabic is *ek* (2nd person)
"love you" / (M/F) *nhebbek*, "tell you" / (M/F) *nkollek*
*In Tunisian, for the first person you always use the prefix 'n' in the simple present tense, for example: *ena nhebbou* / *nhebha*.
*In the Tunisian dialect, the suffix "o" after a verb is intensified to *oo* (e.g., *Nhebboo* instead of *hebbo*).

Conversational Arabic Quick and Easy

House	Dar
In, at, at the	Fi
Car	Karhba
Already	Déja/ ça y est
Good morning	Sbeh el khir
How are you?	Shni ahwelek
Where are you from?	Inti mneen?
Impossible	Mostaheel /impossible
Hello	A'slema
What is your name?	Shesmek / shnou esmek
How old are you?	Kaddesh o'mrek?
Son	Weld
Daughter	Benet
To have	(M) A'ndou / (F) a'nd'ha / (Plur) a'nd'hom
Doesn't *or* **isn't**	Ma
Hard	S'iib (difficult)/ Yebes (solid)
Still	(M) Mazel / (F) Mazelet
Then (or "so")	Ya'ani / donc / I'dhan?

She doesn't have a car, so maybe she is still at the house?
hiyya ma 'a'nd'hesh karhba, ya'ani yomkon hiyya mazelet fil dar?
I am in the car already with your son and daughter
Ena déjà fil karhba m'aa weldek w bentek
Good morning, how are you today?
Sbeh el khir, shni ahwelek el-yoom?
Hello, what is your name?
A'slema, shnou esmek?
How old are you?
Kaddesh o'mrek?
This is very hard, but it's not impossible
Hedha s'iib barsha, ama moosh mostaheel
Then where are you from?
Ya'ani inti mneen?

*In Arabic, possessive pronouns become suffixes to the noun. For example, in the translation for "your," *ek* applies to both, the masculine and the feminine forms:
  "your book" / *ktebek*
  "your house" / *darek*
*In the Arabic language, as well as in other Semitic languages, the article "a" doesn't exist. "She doesn't have a car," *hiya ma a'nd'hesh karhna*.
*Tunisians use French as their second official language, therefore, several words from the French language are incorporated in their native dialect. There is no other form to signify "already", which Tunisians use, except for *déja / ça y est*. The Arabic translation for "impossible" is *mostaheel* however the French variation impossible is used more frequently.

The Program

Thank you	Shokran/ merci
For	Ala khater
Anything	Illi yji / ay haja
That, That is	(M) Hedha / (F) Hedhi
Time	Wakt
But	Ama / Lekin
No/ Not	La / ma/ moosh
I am not	Ena manish
Away	B'eid
Late	Makhar
Similar, like	Yeshbah
Another/ Other	(M) Wehed ehker / ekher (F) wahda okhra / okhra
Side	Jnab / bah'dha/ sheera
Until	Hatta
Yesterday	Emis
Without us	Maghirna
Since	Min
Day	Nhar/yoom
Before	Kbal

Thanks for everything
Shokran ala kol shay
It's almost time
Sar el-wakt takriban
I am not here, I am away
Ena moosh hooni, ena b'eid
That is a similar house
Hedhi dar tshab'helha
I am from the other side
Ena min el-sheera l'okhra
But I was here until late yesterday
Lekin ena kont hooni el-wakt makhar emis
I am not at the other house
Ena moosh fil dar l'okhra

*In Tunisian Arabic, there are two separate cases used to signify "side": *bah'dha* and *sheera*. For "I am from the other side" *sheera*, but for "I stand by your side" here "your side" is *bah'dhek*.
*Negations are expressed as *la, ma,* and *moosh*
"No" / *la*
"I say no" / *Ena nkool la*
Negations preceding the verb are expressed as follows:
"I don't want" / *Ena ma nhebesh*
Expressing negation regarding non-verbs.
Moosh
"This isn't impossible" / *Hedha moosh mostaheel.*
"I am not here" / *Ena moosh hooni.*

I say / I am saying	Nkool / ena nkool
What time is it?	Kaddesh el-wakt taw
I want	Ena nheb
Without you	Min ghirek
Everywhere /wherever	Fil blayes el-kol / fi ay blasa
I am going	Nemshi
With	M'aa
My	Mte'ii *(read footnote)*
Cousin	(S)(M) Wled 'ammi, (F)benet 'ammi /(P) Wled 'ammti, bnet 'ammti
I need	Mohtej / hajti/ lezemni
Right now	Taw/tawa
Night	Leel
To see	Yshoof/ yraa
Light	Dhaw
Outside	El-barra
Without	Min ghir
Happy	Farhan
I see / I am seeing	Nshoof / ena nshoof

I am saying no / I say no
Ena nkool la / nkool la
I want to see this today
Nheb nshouf hedha lyoom
I am with you everywhere
Ena m'aak fil blayes lkol
I am happy without my cousins here
ena ferhan min ghir wled 'ammi hooni
I need to be there at night
Lezemni nkoon ghadi fil leel
I see light outside
Nshouf fi dhaw el-barra
What time is it right now?
Kaddesh el-wakt taw?

*"Mine" / *mte'ii* is a possessive pronoun. *Mte'ii* also means "my" but also becomes a suffix to a noun and it is placed only after a noun. Nouns ending in a vowel end with *–ti*. Nouns ending with a consonant end with *–i*. For example:
"cousin" / *weld 'amm*, "my cousin" / *weld 'ammi*, "cup" / *kess*, "my cup" / *kessi*
For second and third person masculine noun, *weld* ("son"), male and female (S) *ek*, (P) *kom*. "His" – *mte'oo*/ "hers" – *mte'ha*, noun endings will be *o* (for male) and *a* (for female).
"your son" / (m. and f.) *weldek*, "your (plural) son" / (m. and f.) *wledkom*, "his son" / *weldo*, "her son" / *weld'ha*, "our son" / *weldna*, "their son" / *weld'hom*
For second and third person feminine noun: "car" / *karhba*.
"your car" / *karhabtek*, "your (plural) car" / *karhbetkom*, "his car" / *karhabto*, "her car" / *karhbet'ha*,"our car" / *karhbetna*, "their car" / *karhbet'hom*

*This *isn't* a phrase book! The purpose of this book is solely to provide you with the tools to create *your own* sentences!

The Program

Place	Blasa
Easy	Sehel
To find	Yelka
To look for/to search	Ylawwej
Near / Close	Kreeb
To wait	Yestanna
To sell	Ybi'i
To use	Ystaa'mill
To know	Yaa'ref
To decide	Ykarrer
Between	Mabin
Both	Ezzouz
To	L'
Next to	Janb/ bahdha

This place it's easy to find
Hedhi blasa sehel besh telkaha
I want to look for this next to the car
Nheb nlawwej ala hedha bahdha el-karhba
I am saying to wait until tomorrow
Ena nkoul nistanew hatta l'ghodwa
This table is easy to sell
Hedhi tawla sehel besh tbii'ha
I want to use this
Nheb nista'mil hedhi (or hedha for m.)
I need to know where is the house
Nheb na'aref el-dar ween mawjouda
I want to decide between both places
Nheb nkkarer mabin ezzouz blayes

*Please pay close attention to the conjugation of verbs, whether they are in first person, second, or third. Unlike Anglo-Germanic languages, Latin languages, or even Classical Arabic, in which the first verb is conjugated and the following is always infinitive, in colloquial Arabic, it is quite different. The first verb is conjugated and the following one is conjugated as well. Keep in mind: The Tunisian dialect of the Arabic language is considered a colloquial, rather than an official language.

Because	Khater / 'ala-khater
To buy	Yeshri
Life	'Omr, hayet
Them, they, their	Lihom/ hooma/ mt'ehom
Bottle	Dabbouza
Book	Kteb
Mine	Lili/ liya/ mt'eii
To understand	Yefhem
Problem / Problems	(S) Moshkla/ (P) Mashekil
I do / I am doing	Naa'mel / ena naa'mel
Of	Mte'i
To look	Yshouf/ yraa
Myself	Ena
Enough	Yakfi / yezzi
Food / water	Mekla / ma
Each/ every/ entire/ all	El-kol / kolhom/ jm'ii
Hotel	Outil/ hotel

I like this hotel because I want to look at the beach
Y'ejbni hedha l outil khater nheb nshouf el-shatt
I want to buy a bottle of water
Nheb neshri dabbouza ma
I do this every day
Na'amel hedha kol yoom
Both of them have enough food
Ezouz 'anhdom mekla takfi
That is the book, and that book is mine
Hedha howa el-kteb, w hedha el-kteb mte'ii
I need to understand the problem
Ena lezimni nefhem el-moshkla
I see the view of the city from the hotel
Nshouf mandher el-mdina mil hotel
I do my homework today
Ena na'amil droosi lyoom
My entire life (all my life)
'Omri kemil

*There are two ways of saying "life" in Arabic: *'omr* and *hayet*.

The Program

I like	Nheeb/ ye'jebni
There is / There are	Famma
Family / Parents	'Ayla / waldin
Why	'Alesh
To say	Ykoul
Something	Haja
To go	Yemshi
Ready	Hadher
Soon	Kreeb / ala kreeb
To work	Yekhdem
Who	Shkoon / illi
Busy	Mashghool
That (conjunction)	(m) Anno / (f) anha
I Must	Lezem
Important	Mouhemma

I like to be at my house with my parents
Ena nheb nkoon fi dari m'aa waldiya
I want to know why I need to say something important
Nheb na'aref 'alesh lezimni nkool haja mouhemma
I am there with him
Ena ghadi m'aah
I am busy, but I need to be ready soon
Ena mashghool, ama lezimni nahdhar ala kreeb
I like to go to work
Nheb nemshi lel khedma
'Who is there?
Shkoon ghadi?
I want to know if they are here, because I want to go outside
Nheb na'aref hooma hooni walla, khater nheb nokhrej
There are seven dolls
Famma sab'aa lou'ab
I need to know that it is a good idea
Nheb na'aref anha fekra behya

*In the last sentence, we use "that" as a conjunction (*anha*).

How much /How many	Kaddesh
To bring	Yjeeb
With me	M'aaya
Instead	Fi 'oudh
Only	Kahaw/ kein
When	Wakt
I can / Can I?	Najjem / najjem?
Or	Aw/walla
Were	Kenoo
Without me	Maghiri / min ghiri
Fast	Fisaa'
Slow	Beshwaya
Cold	Bered
Inside	El-dekhil
To eat	Yekil
Hot	Skhoun
To Drive	Ysook

How much money do I need to bring with me?
Kaddesh floos lezimni njeeb m'aaya
Instead of this cake, I want that cake
Fi 'oudh hal gateau, nheb hal gateau
Only when you can
Kein wakt tnajjem
They were without me yesterday
Kenoo min ghiri ames
Do I need to drive the car fast or slow?
Lezimni nsook el-karhba fisaa' walla beshwaya
It is cold inside the library
Famma bard fi west lmaktba
Yes, I like to eat this hot for my lunch
Ayh, nheb neekil hedha skhoun fi ftouri
I can work today
Najjem nekhdem el-yoom

*"Were" is *kenoo*, "we were" is *konna*.

The Program

To answer	Yjeweb
To fly	Yteer / ysefer *(read the footnote please)*
Time / Times	Marra / Marrat
To travel	Ysefer
To learn	Yt'aallem
How	Kifesh
To swim	Y'oom
To practice	Yitmarren/ yetdarreb
To play	Yel'aab
To leave (something)	Ykhalli
Many /much /a lot	Barsha
I go to	Nemshi 'ala khater/besh
First	Awwel
To leave (a place)	Yemshi
Around	Hawl

I want to answer many questions
Nheb njeweb 'ala barsha as'ila
I must fly to Dubai today
Lezem nsafer el-Dubai lyoom
I need to learn how to swim at the pool
Lezemni nit'aalem kifesh n'oom fil piscine
I want to learn to play better tennis
Nheb nit'aalm nil'ab tennis ahsan
I want to leave this here for you when I go to travel the world
Nheb nkhalli hedha hooni leek wakt nemshi nsaefer hawl l'aalam
Since the first time
Min awwel marra
The children are yours
Esghar sgharek inti

*In Arabic there are 3 definitions for time:
-Time, *wakt* refers to; era, moment period, duration of time.
-Time(s), *marra*(t) refers to; occasion or frequency.
-Time, *se'aa* in reference to; hour, what time is it.
-* There are two forms of the word fly:
-"To fly" (like birds do) *yteer*;
-"To take flight" / *ysefer*.
*With the knowledge you've gained so far, now try to create *your own* sentences!

Nobody / Anyone	Hatta had / had
Against	Dhodd/ 'aks
Us	Ahna
To visit	Yzoor
Mom / Mother	Mama, ommi
To give	Yaa'ti
Which	Anehou / illi
To meet	Ykabel
Someone	Had
Just	Kahaw/juste
To walk	Yemshi
Week	Jom'aa
Towards	Bittijehh
Than	Min
Nothing	Hatta shay

Something is better than nothing
Haja khir min blesh
I am against him
Ena dhoddo
Is there anyone here?
Famma shkoun hoon?
We go to visit my family each week
Ahna nemshiw ntollo ala l'ayla kol jom'aa
I need to give you something
Nheb naa'tik haja
Do you want to go meet someone?
T'hebshi temshi tkabel hadd?
I was here on Wednesdays as well
Ena kont hooni nhar lerb'aa zeda
Do you do this everyday?
Inti taa'mel hakka kol yoom?
You need to walk around, but not towards the house
Inti lezmek taa'mel doora, ama moosh bittijeh el-dar

*In Arabic, when using the pronoun "you" as a direct and indirect object pronoun (the person who is actually affected by the action that is being carried out) in relation to a verb, the pronoun "you" becomes a suffix to that verb. That suffix becomes *ik* (masc.) *ek* (fem.). For example: "to give" / *yaa'ti*: "to give you" / *besh naa'tik*, "to tell" / *ykool*: "to tell you" / *besh nkollek* (m.), *qoolik* (f.), "to see" / *shoof*, "see you" / *yshoofek*: "to see you" (plural) / *nshoofkom* (m.), *shoofkan* (f.).

For third person male, add *o* and *om* for plural, for female add *ha* and *om* for plural. For example: "tell him" / *kollo*, "tell her" / *kolha*, "see them" / *shoofhom* (m.), *shoofhen* (f.), "see us "/ *shoofna*.

*There are two forms of the word "which" in Tunisian Arabic:
"Which one?" / *Anehou*
"Which proves that" / *illi*

The Program

I have	'Andi
Don't	Ma
Friend	Saheb, sadeek
To borrow	Yetsallef
To look like / resemble	Yeshbah
Grandfather	Jaddi
To want	Yheb
To stay	Yok'od
To continue	Ykammill
That's why	Heka
Way	Kayyes/ sheraa'/ treek
I don't	Manish
To show	Yetfarrej
To prepare	Yhadher
I am not going	Ena manish meshi

Do you want to look like Salim?
Theb twalli tshabah Salim?
I want to borrow this book for my grandfather
Ena nheb nitsallef hedha el-kteb l'jaddi
I want to drive and to continue on this way to my house
Ena nheb nkammel nsook fi hedha el-treek hatta noosil lil dar
I have a friend there, that's why I want to stay in Sfax
'Andi saheb ghadi, heka alesh nheb nok'od fi Sfax
I am not going to see anyone here
Manish besh nshoof hatta had hooni
I need to show you how to prepare breakfast
Lezemni nwarrik kifesh t'hadhdher ftoor esbeh
Why don't you have the book?
Alesh ma 'andeksh el-kteb?
That is incorrect, I don't need the car today
Hedha ghalet, mahajtish bil karhba el-yoom

To remember	Yetfakker
Your	Mte'ik
Number	Rakm / noomru
Hour	Se'aa
Dark / darkness	Dhlam
About / on the	'La/ hawl/ fi
Grandmother	Jadti
Five	Khamsa
Minute / Minutes	Dkika/ dkayak
More	Akther
To think	Yfakker / ykhammem
To do	Yaa'mel
To come	Yji
To hear	Yesmaa'
Last	Ekher
To talk / To Speak	Yetkallam / yahki

You need to remember my number
Lezmek titfakker rakmi
This is the last hour of darkness
Hedhi ekher se'aa mte' dhlam
I want to come and to hear my grandmother speak Arabic
Ena nheb nji w nesmaa' jadti tahki bil 'arbi
I need to think more about this, and what to do
Nheb nfakker akther fil sujet hedha, w shnu naa'mel
From here to there, it's only five minutes
Min hooni l'ghadi, juste khamsa dkayak
The school on the mountain
El-madrsa fil jbal

*In Arabic with the question "is it?", the "it" can pertain to either a masculine or feminine noun. However, whenever pertaining to a masculine or feminine noun, it will become *howa* or *hiya*. For example, when referring to a feminine noun such as *karhba* ("the car"), "is it (the car in question) here?" / *hiya hooni?* When referring to a masculine noun such as *kalb* ("a dog"), "is it (the dog in question) on the table?" *howa ala tawla?* For neuter, it's *hedha*. However, I yet again wish to stress that this isn't a grammar book!

The Program

Early	Bekri
Tunisia	Tunes
Again	Marra okhra
Arabic	Arabi
To take	Yekhodh
To try	Yjarreb/ hawel
To rent	Yekri
Without her	Min ghirha
We are	Ahna
To turn off	Ytaffi/ ysakker
To ask	Yis'al/ yotlob
To stop	Ywakkef
Permission	Edhn
While	Fatra/zaman

He needs to leave and rent a house at the beach
Lezmo yemshi w yekri dar 'ala el-shatt
I want to take the test without her
Ena nheb nekhedh el-test min ghirha
We are here a long time
Ahna hooni min modda
I need to turn off the lights early tonight
Lezemni ntaffi el-dhawet bekri ellila
We want to stop here
Ahna lezemna nekfu hooni
We are from Sousse
Ahna min Sousse
The same building
Nafs el-banya
I want to ask permission to leave
Nheb notlob l'edhn besh nokhroj

Conversational Arabic Quick and Easy

To open	Yhell
A bit, a little, a little bit	Shwayya
To pay	Yidfaa'
Once again	Marra okhra
There isn't/ there aren't	Mafammesh
Sister	Okht
To hope	Yitmanna
To live (to exist)	Y'eesh
To live (in a place)	Yaskun
Nice to meet you	Tsharaft bmaa'reftek
Name	Ism
Last name	Lakab
To return	Yarjaa'
America	Amarica
Door	Beb

I need to open the door for my sister
Lezemni nhel el-beb l'okhti
I need to buy something
Lezemni neshri haja
I want to meet your sisters
Nheb nkabel okhtek
Nice to meet you, what is your name and your last name?
Tsharraft b maa'reftek, shnu el-esm w el-lakab mte'ik
To hope for a little better
Nitmanna shay ahsan
I want to return from the United States and to live in Qatar without problems
Nheb narjaa' min Amarica w nheb noskon fi Qatar maghir mashekill
Why are you sad right now?
(M)alesh mitghashesh tawa? (F) alesh mitghashesha tawa?
There aren't any people here
Mafamma hatta had hooni
There isn't enough time to go to Djebra today
Mafamesh wakt kefi besh temshi l'djerba lyoom

*In Tunisian Arabic, regarding the verb "to meet," there are two separate cases to define this verb: *tejtema'* and *kabil*, depending of the context. To meet for business is *tejtema'*. To meet for getting acquainted is *kabil*. In the sentence, "Do you want to go meet someone?" (the sister, getting acquainted with her), it's *kabil*.

*This *isn't* a phrase book! The purpose of this book is *solely* to provide you with the tools to create *your own* sentences!

The Program

To happen	Yseer
To order	Yotlob
To drink	Yeshrob
Excuse me	Samahni/ naa'tadhir
Child	(M) Ebn/ weld, (F) Bint
Woman	M'ra
To begin / To start	Yebda
To finish	Ykammel / yoofa
To help	Y'aawen
To smoke	Yetkayyef
To love	Yheb
Afternoon	El-kayla

This must happen today
Hedha lezem ysir el-yoom
Excuse me, my child is here as well
Samahni, weldi/benti hooni zeda
I love you
Ena nhebek
I see you
Nshoof fik
I need you at my side
Hajti bik m'aaya
I need to begin soon to be able to finish at 3 o'clock in the afternoon
Lezemni nebda ala kreeb besh najjem nkammel tletha mte' el-kayla
I need help
Hajti b'muse'ada
I don't want to smoke once again
Ma nhebesh netkayyef marra okhra
I want to learn how to speak Arabic
Nheb nit'aallem nahki bil 'arbi

*"To help" is 'aawen. However, "help!" is muse'ada. "I need help" or "I need rescue" /ena hajti b muse'ada.

Conversational Arabic Quick and Easy

To read	Yakra
To write	Yekteb
To teach	Y'aallem
To close	Ysakker
To choose	Yakhtar
To prefer	Yfadhal/ ykhayyar
To put	Yhott
Less	Akal
Sun	Shams
Month	Sh'har
I Talk	Nahki/netkallem
Exact	Shih / bil dhabt

I need this book to learn how to read and write in Arabic because I want to teach in Egypt
Hajti bel kteb hedha besh nit'aallem nakra w nekteb bil 'arbi khater nheb nkarri fi Masr
I want to close the door of the house
Lezemni nsakker beb el-dar
I prefer to put the gift here
Nkhayyer nhott el-hadiya hooni
I want to pay less than you for the dinner
Nheb nedfaa' akal mennek fil 'asha
I speak with the boy and the girl in French
Netkallem m'aa tfol wel tofla bel Français
There is sun outside today
Famma shams el-barra el-yoom
Is it possible to know the exact date?
Momken naa'ref el-date bil dhabt?
Where is the airport
Ween el-matar?
I need to go to sleep now
Lezemni nemshi norkod tawa

*"For the" is *l'*
*"In" is *bil*
*With the knowledge you've gained so far, now try to create your own sentences!

To exchange (*money*)	Ysarraf
To call	Yotlob
Brother	Khu
Dad	Bu
To sit	Yok'od
Together	M'aa b'adhna
To change	Ybaddel
Of course	Akeed / bien sur
Welcome	Ahla/ marhba
During	Wakt
Year/Years	(S)'Am/sna/(P)a'wem/sneen
Sky	Sma
Up	Fook
Down	Loota
Sorry	Samahni/naa'tadher
To follow	Ytabba' /yelhak
To the	Ila / lil / l'
Big	Kbeer
New	Jdeed
Never / ever	Abadan/marra okhra/jemla

I don't want to exchange this money at the bank
Ma nhebesh nsarraf hal floos fil banka
I want to call my brother and my dad today
Ena nheb nkallem khuya w buya lyoom
Of course I can come to the theater, and I want to sit together with you and with your sister
Akeed najjem nji lil masrah, w nheb nok'od bahdhek w bahdha okhtek
I need to go down to see your new house
Lezemni nahbat loota besh nshoof darek el-jdida
I can see the sky from the window
Najjem nshoof el-sma mil shobbeik
I am sorry, but he wants to follow her to the store
Naa'tadher, ama yheb ytabbaa'ha lil hanoot
I don't ever want to see you again
Ma nhebesh nshoofek marra okhra

*In Tunisian dialect, brother is *khu*, and dad is *bu*. However, "my dad" is *buya* and "my brother" is *khuya*. "My sister" is *okhti*, and "my mother" is *ommi*.
*For the possessive pronouns, her (*ha*) and him (*o*), both become suffixes to the verb or noun. Concerning nouns: her house / *darha*, his house / *daro*, concerning cases regarding verbs, please see footnotes on page 120.

To allow	Ykhalli
To believe	Ysaddak
Morning	Sbeh
Except	Bekhlef / appart
To promise	You'ed
Good night	Tisbah 'ala khir
Each	Kol
People	Ness / 'abed
To move (an object)	Yhawwel
To move (to a place)	Yhawwel
Far	B'eid
Different	Mokhtalef/ moosh kif/mbaddel
Man	Rajel
To enter	Yodkhol
To receive	Yestalam/ yekhodh/yekbel
Quickly	Fisa' fisa'
Good evening	Nharek zin / Bonsoir
Left / right	Y'sar / ymeen
Street	Kayyes/ nahj/ sheraa'

I need to allow him to go with us, he is a different man now
Lezemni nkhallih yemshi m'aana, howa taw rajel mokhtalef
I believe everything except this
Nsaddak kol shay bikhlef hedha
I promise to say good night to my parents each night
Noo'ed besh nkool tesbah 'ala khir l'waldiya kol lila
The people from Jordan are very pleasant
El-ness li mil Ordon behyeen barsha
I need to find another hotel very quickly
Lezmeni nilka hotel ekher fisa' fisa'
They need to receive a book for work
Lezemhom yestalmu kteb lil khedma
I see the sun in the morning
Nshoof el-shams fil sbeh
The house is on the right side of the street
El-dar 'ala ysar el-sheraa'

*There are two forms of the word "except"/ *bekhlef* and *appart*. *Appart* is the commonly used French variation.

The Program

To wish	Yetmanna
Bad	Mshoom/ khayeb
To Get	Yekhodh / yekhu
To forget	Yensa
Everybody / Everyone	Kolhom/ kol had / el-kol
Although	Raghm/raghm annu/pourtant
To feel	Yhess
Past	Madhi
Next (following, after)	Ejey
To like	Yheb / ye'ijeb
In front	Koddem
Next (near, close)	Bahdha / b'jnab
Behind	W'ra
Well	Labes
Goodbye	Bye/ bislema
Restaurant	Mat'aam/resto/restaurant
Bathroom	Salle de bain/toilette/beet el-banu

I don't want to wish you anything bad
Ena ma nhebesh nitmanelek ay shay khayeb
I must forget everybody from my past to feel well
Lezemni nensa kol had min el-madhi mte'i besh nhes labes
I am next to the person behind you
Ena b'jnab eshakhs li w'rak
There is a great person in front of me
Famma shakhs heyel koddemi
I say goodbye to my friends
Ena nkool bislema l's'habee
Where is the bathroom in the restaurant?
Ween e-toilette fil resto?
She has to get a car before the next year
Lezemha tekhu karhba kbal 'am ejjey
I like the house, but it is very small
E'ijbetni el dar, ama hiya sgheera barsha

*Bahdha literally means "side." In Tunisian Arabic, it refers to "next." *Bahdheya* is "besides me" and *bahdhek* is "besides you."
*There are three forms of the word "restaurant" / *mat'aam, resto,* and *restaurant* (in French).
*There are two forms of the word "although" / *raghm, raghm annu,* and *pourtant* (in French).
*There are three forms of the word "bathroom" / *salle de bain* (in French, and most commonly used), *toilette, beet el-banu*.

Conversational Arabic Quick and Easy

To remove / to take out	Ynahhi
Please	Y'ayshek/min fadhlek/ billehi/ta'mel mzeyya
Beautiful	(M)Mizyein, (F)mizyeina
To lift	Yhez
Include / Including	Bima fi dhelek / b'ei'tibar
Belong	Tebaa'/ mte'
To hold	Yshed/yhez
To check	Yet'aked/ ythabbet
Small	Sgheer
Real	Hakiki/ berrsmi
Weather	Jom'aa/ osboo'
Size	Kobr/ hajm
High	Irtifa'
Doesn't	Moosh
So (as in then)	Yaa'ni
So (as in very)	Barsha / yecer *(please read footnote below)*
Price	Soom / prix (in French)
Correct	S'heeh

She wants to remove this door please
T'heb tnahhi hedha el-beb y'ayshek
This doesn't belong here, I need to check again
Hedhi moosh teb'aa l'hooni, lezemni nthabet marra okhra
This week the weather was very beautiful
Hal jom'aa taks kein mizyein barsha
I need to know which is the real diamond
Lezemni naa'ref ama hiya el-jawhara el-hakikiya
We need to check the size of the house
Lezemna nthabtu fi kobr el-dar
I want to lift this, so you need to hold it high
Nheb nhez hedhi, donc lezmek t'shed'ha lfook
I can pay this even though that the price is expensive
Najjem nedfaa' hak'ha pourtant soom ghali
Including everything is this price correct?
B'ei'tibar kol-shay, el-prix s'heeh?

*The word "so" translates into *barsha / yecer* and, unlike in English, it is placed after the adjective.

Countries of the Middle East
Bildan el-sharq el-awsatt

Lebanon	Lobnen
Syria	Soorya
Jordan	L'ordon
Israel/Palestine	Isra'eel / filasteen
Iraq	El-Irak
Saudi Arabia	Sa'odiyya
Kuwait	El-Kweit
Qatar	Qatar
Bahrain	El-Bahrein
United Arab Emirates	El-emarat
Oman	'Oman
Yemen	El-Yaman
Egypt	Masr
Libya	Leebya
Tunisia	Tunes
Algeria	Dzzeyir
Morocco	El-Maghreb

Months

January	Janvee
February	Fivree
March	Mars
April	Avreel
May	Mei
June	Jwan
July	Jwilya
August	Oot
September	Septembre
October	Octobre
November	Novembre
December	Décembre

Days of the Week

Sunday	Ahad
Monday	Thnein
Tuesday	Tleith
Wednesday	Erb'aa
Thursday	Khmees
Friday	Jem'aa
Saturday	Sabt

Seasons

Spring	Rabee'
Summer	Seif
Autumn	Khreef
Winter	Shta

Cardinal Directions

North	Shameil
South	Janoob
East	Shark
West	Gharb

Colors

Black	(M)Akhal (F)kahla
White	(M)Abyedh (F) Beidha
Gray	(M)Gri (F) gri
Red	(M)Ahmer (F)Hamra
Blue	(M)Azrek(F)Zarka
Yellow	(M)Asfer (F)Safra
Green	(M)Akhder (F)Khadra
Orange	Bortoukali
Purple	Mauve
Brown	(M)Bonni (F)Bonniyya

Numbers

One	Wehid
Two	Thnein
Three	Tletha
Four	Arb'aa
Five	Khamsa
Six	Sitta
Seven	Sab'aa
Eight	Thmanya
Nine	Tis'aa
Ten	'Ashra

Twenty	'Eshreen
Thirty	Tletheen
Forty	Arb'een
Fifty	Khamseen
Sixty	Sitteen
Seventy	Saba'een
Eighty	Thmeneen
Ninety	Tisi'in
Hundred	Miyya
Thousand	Alf
Million	Malyoon

Conversational
Arabic Quick
and Easy

ALGERIAN DIALECT

YATIR NITZANY

THE ALGERIAN DIALECT

Out of the estimated forty million people who live in Algeria (2016), around 75% to 80% speak Algerian Arabic, or Algerian (known as Darja or Dziria) as their first language, and another 20% speak it as a second language.

Algerian is a language derived from a variety of Arabic languages spoken in northern Algeria. It belongs to the Maghrebi Arabic language continuum and is mutually understandable with Tunisian and Moroccan Arabic.

Like other varieties of Maghrebi Arabic, Algerian dialects have a mostly Semitic vocabulary, with significant under-layers and numerous loanwords from French, Ottoman Turkish, and Spanish.

Just like Moroccan Arabic (Darija), Algerian Arabic includes several distinct dialects with some belonging to two genetically different groups: pre-Hilalian and Hilalian dialects.

Pre-Hilalian dialects are a consequence of the early Arabization phases of the Maghreb, from the 7th to the 12th centuries, concerning the main urban settlements, the harbors, the religious centers (zaouias), and the main trade routes.

Algerian Arabic is essentially a spoken language used in daily communication and entertainment, while Classical Arabic is generally reserved for official use and education.

Spoken in: Algeria

ARABIC PRONUNCIATIONS

PLEASE MASTER THE FOLLOWING PAGE IN ARABIC PRONUNCIATIONS PRIOR TO STARTING THE PROGRAM

Kha. For Middle Eastern languages including Arabic, Hebrew, Farsi, Pashto, Urdu, Hindi, etc., and also German, to properly pronounce the kh or ch is essential, for example, *Khaled* (a Muslim name) or *Chanukah* (a Jewish holiday) or *Nacht* ("night" in German). The best way to describe kh or ch is to say "ka" or "ha" while at the same time putting your tongue at the back of your throat and blowing air. It's pronounced similarly to the sound that you make when clearing your throat. Please remember this whenever you come across any word containing a kh in this program.

Ghayin. The Arabic gh is equivalent to the "g" in English, but its pronunciation more closely resembles the French "r," rather than "g." Pronounce it at the back of your throat. The sound is equivalent to what you would make when gargling water. Gha is pronounced more as "rha," rather than as "ga." *Ghada* is pronounced as "rhada." In this program, the symbol for *ghayin* is gh, so keep your eyes peeled.

Aayin is pronounced as a'a, pronounced deep at the back of your throat. Rather similar to the sound one would make when gagging. In the program, the symbol for *aayin* is a'a, u'u, o'o, or i'i.

Ha is pronounced as "ha." Pronunciation takes place deep at the back of your throat, and for correct pronunciation, one must constrict the back of the throat and exhale air while simultaneously saying "ha." In the program, this strong h ("ha") is emphasized whenever *ha, ah, hi, he,* or *hu* is encountered.

NOTE TO THE READER

The purpose of this book is merely to enable you to communicate in the Algerian Arabic dialect. In the program itself (pages 17-38) you may notice that the composition of some of those sentences might sound rather clumsy. This is intentional. These sentences were formulated in a specific way to serve two purposes: to facilitate the easy memorization of the vocabulary and to teach you how to combine the words in order to form your own sentences for quick and easy communication, rather than making complete literal sense in the English language. So keep in mind that this is not a phrase book!

As the title suggests, the sole purpose of this program is for conversational use only. It is based on the mirror translation technique. These sentences, as well as the translations are not incorrect, just a little clumsy. Latin languages, Semitic languages, and Anglo-Germanic languages, as well as a few others, are compatible with the mirror translation technique.

Many users say that this method surpasses any other known language learning technique that is currently out there on the market. Just stick with the program and you will achieve wonders!

Note to the Reader

Again, I wish to stress this program is by no means, shape, or form a phrase book! The sole purpose of this book is to give you a fundamental platform to enable you to connect certain words to become conversational. Please also read the "Introduction" and the "About Me" section prior to commencing the program.

In order to succeed with my method, please start on the very first page of the program and fully master one page at a time prior to proceeding to the next. Otherwise, you will overwhelm yourself and fail. Please do not skip pages, nor start from the middle of the book.

It is a myth that certain people are born with the talent to learn a language, and this book disproves that myth. With this method, anyone can learn a foreign language as long as he or she follows these explicit directions:

* Memorize the vocabulary on each page

* Follow that memorization by using a notecard to cover the words you have just memorized and test yourself.

* Then read the sentences following that are created from the vocabulary bank that you just mastered.

* Once fully memorized, give yourself the green light to proceed to the next page.

Again, if you proceed to the following page without mastering the previous, you are guaranteed to gain nothing from this book. If you follow the prescribed steps, you will realize just how effective and simplistic this method is.

THE PROGRAM

Let's Begin! *"Vocabulary"*
(memorize the vocabulary)

I | I am	Ana / ani | rani
With you	(Masc) Ma'ak nta/ (Fem) Ma'ak nti
With him / with her	(M) Ma'ah (F) ma'aha
With us	Ma'ana
For you	Lik
Without him / her	(Masc) Bla bih / (F) Bla biha
Without them	Bla beehoum
Always	Daymen
Was	Kan
This, This is, it is	(M) Hada / (F) hady
Today	El-yom
Sometimes	Myndek
Maybe	Balek
You	(M) Nta / (F) nti / (plural) ntouma
Are you, you are	(M) Rak / (F) Raki / (P) Rakoum
He/ he is	Huwa
She/ she is	Hiya
From	Men / from where - Mnin
Better	Khir min

Sentences composed from the vocabulary (now you can speak the sentences and combine the words).

This is for you
Hada Lik
I am from Algeria
Ana men dzayer
Are you from Algiers?
Enta men dzayer?
I am with you
Ana ma'ak

Sometimes you are with us at the mall
Mindek rak ma'ana f'centre commercial
I am always with her
Ana daymen ma'aha
Are you without them today?
Rak bla beehom el-yom?
Sometimes I am with him
Mindek rani ma'ah

*In Algerian Arabic, there are gender rules. Saying "for you" to a male is *lik nta*, but if you are talking to a female, it's *lik nti*.
*To indicate "with him"/ "with her," we use (M) *ma'ah* / (F) *ma'aha*. However, the forms *mâ'ah howa* /*mâ'aha hya* may be used as well to indicate "with him" or "with her."
*In Algerian Arabic, "with you" is *ma'ak nta*, *ma'ak nti*; however, *rana kif kif* may be used as well. *Rana ma' ba'ad* is basically an expression used to indicate "we are together."

I was	Ana kunt
To be	(M) Tkun / (F) tkouni
The	El
Same / same thing	Kif kif
Good	Mlih
Here	Hna
Very	Bezaaf
And	Wa
Between	Ma bin
Now	Douka
Later / After / afterwards	Men ba'ad/Aprés (french)
If	Lookan
Yes	Ih
To	L'
Tomorrow	Ghadwa
Day	Yom
Also / too / as well	Tani

If it's between now and later
Loukan tkoun ma bin douka w men ba'ad
It's better tomorrow
Khir ghadwa
This is good as well
(F) hadi mliha tani (M) hada mlih tani
To be the same person
Tkoon nafss el chakhss
Yes, you are very good
Ih, nta mlih bezaaf
I was here with them
Ana kunt hna ma'ahom
You and I
(M) Nta w ana /(F) nti w ana
The same day
Nafss el yom

*Keep in mind that the Algerian Arabic dialect is heavily influenced by the French language.
*In Algerian dialect "I Was" is *ana kount*
He was - *houwa kan*
She was- *hiya kanet*
We were- *hna kouna*

Me	Li (read footnote)
Ok	Ok
Even if	Hatta loukan
No	Lala
Worse	Ayane
Where	Win
Everything	Koolech
Somewhere	F kach plassa
What	Wechnoo?
Almost	Qrib
There	Temma
Is it?	(M)Had? / (F)hadi? *(footnote)*

Afterwards is worse
Men ba'ad ayane ktar
Even if I go now
Hatta law kan nroh dooka
Where is everything?
Win rahoo koulesh?
Maybe somewhere
Balek f kash plassa
What? I am almost there
Wechnoo? rani qrib nalhaq
Where are you?
(M) win rak? / (F) win raki?
Where is the airport?
Win l'airoport?

*"There" has two meanings, so it is *kayna* or *temma*, depending on the context. When we say "there is" we say *kayn* / but when we say "I am there" (place) we say *rani temma*.
* *F'el plassa* literally means "in a place."
* In Arabic, the pronoun "me" has several definitions. In relation to verbs it's *li*. *Li* refers to any verb that relates to the action of doing something to someone or for someone. For example, "tell me," "tell (to) me" / *qol li*.
'Alay just means "me": "love me" / *habni*
Other variations (*ya*):
-"on me" / *'aliya*, "in me" / *fiya*
-"to me" / *'liya*, "with me" / *ma'aya*
-"in front of me" / *ganby*, "from me" / *hadaya*
The same rule applies for "him" and "her"—both become suffixes: *–h* and *–ha*. Basically all verbs pertinent to males end with *h*, and all pertinent to female end with *ha*.
-"love her" / *habha*, "love him" / *habih*, "love them" / *habhoum* , "love us" / *habouna*.
* Any verb that relates to doing something to someone, or for someone put *l*:
-"tell her" / *qol-lha*, "tell him" / *qol-lou*, "tell them" / *qol-lelhoum*, "tell us" /*qol-lelna*
* In Algerian Arabic to signify "love" we can either use *heb* or *moot 'ala*.
*In Arabic with the question "is it?", *had* the "it" is used to describe both female and masculine noun but it could be also replaced by *hadi* for a female or *hada* for a male and for plural we use *hadou*. For example, when referring to a feminine noun such as *tomobil* or *corossa* ("the car"), "is it (the car in question) yours?" *hadi corossa dyalek?* When referring to a masculine noun such as *el kaleb* ("a dog"), "is it (the dog in question) yours" *had el kelb dyalek?*

House	Dar
In / at	Dakhel / fel / lel
Car	Tomobil / corossa
Already	Déjà (French)
Good morning	Sabah el kheir
How are you?	(M) Wechrak / (F) Wechraky
Where are you from?	(M) Mninek/minek nta (F) mninek/minek nti
Impossible	Mustaheel / impossible
Hello	Ahlan
What is your name?	Wesmek?
How old are you?	(M) Sh-hal fi 'omrak?
Son	Wlad
Daughter	Bent
To have	(M) Endo / (F) 'Endaha
Doesn't	Ma
Hard	S'eeb
Still	(M) Mazal / (F) Mazalha
Then (or "so")	Men ba'ad / ya'any / alors (French)
With	Ma'a

She doesn't have a car, so maybe she is still at the house?
Heya ma'andheshe tomobil, Alors balek mazalha f'dar?
I am in the car already with your son and daughter
Ana fel tomobil déja ma'a wlidak w bentak
Good morning, how are you today?
Sabah el kheir, wechrak el-yom?
Hello, what is your name?
Ahlan, wasmak?
How old are you?
Sh-hal f'omrak?
This is very hard, but it's not impossible
Hada s'eeb bezaaf, bsah machi mustaheel/impossible
Then where are you from?
Ya'any mninek nta/nti?

*In Arabic, possessive pronouns become suffixes to the noun. For example, in the translation for "your," *ak* is the masculine form, and *ik* is the feminine form.
-"your book" / *ktabak (m.), ktabik (f.)*
-"your house" / *darak (m.), darik (f.)*

*In Algerian Arabic, in the event that "doesn't" is used regarding negations of verbs, the following requirements must precede and follow *ma kat'* ... *esh*, for example: "she doesn't like the lemonade" (The verb "like" is *ajab*) – *heya ma'ya'aajbhashe el gazouz*.

*"Where are you from" is (M) *mnein nta?* (F) *mnein nti?* However, (M) *mn fein nta?* / (F) *mn fein nti?* may be used as well.

The Program

Thank you	Shukran / ya'atik saha
For	L' / aala
Anything	Ay haja
That / That is	Hadik
Time	Sa'a *(see footnote below)*
But	Bssah / Wa lakin
No / Not	La' / mashy
I am not	Ana mashy / maranish
Away	B'eed / Barra
Late	La'achya
Similar	Kif kif
Another/ Other	Wahed lukher
Side	Jiha / coté (French)
Until	Htta el
Yesterday	Bareh
Without us	Bla bina
Since	Melli
Day	Yom
Before	Qbel

Thanks for everything
Shukran aala koolch / koolchi
It's almost time
Qrib el wakt
I am not here, I am away
Ana maranish hena, rani bara/b'eed
That is a similar house
Had el dar kif kif
I am from the other side
Ana men el-jiha el-okhra
But I was here until late yesterday
Bssah ana koont hna hatta elbareh la'achiya
I am not at the other house
Ana maranish fi el-dar el okhra

*In Algerian Arabic, there are three definitions for time:
-"time" / *mudda* refers to "moment period," "duration of time."
-"time(s)" / *marra(t)* / *karra(t)* refers to "occasion" or "frequency."
-"time" / *sa'a* references "hour," "what time is it?"

*In Algerian Arabic, with negations such as "no," "not," "doesn't," "can't," and "don't," use either *mashy* or *lala*. *Lala* is used to indicate cases such as "are you here" – *Rak hna* – and you then reply "no," *lala*. *Ma ranich hna* is used to indicate cases of "not," "doesn't," or "don't," for example: "I am not at the other house" is *ma ranish f'dar el okhra*.

Conversational Arabic Quick and Easy

I say / I am saying	Ana qolt / Rani nkool
What time is it?	Sh-hal sa'a?
I want	Habeet or "M" Ani hab / "F" Ani habba
Without you	Bla beek
Everywhere /wherever	F'kool plasse / partout (French)
I go	Ana nrouh
My	Dyalli / ta'ee
Cousin	Cousin (paternal) - (M) Wlid 'amy / (F) bent 'amy / (P) (M) wlaad 'amy / (P)(F) bnaat 'amy / Cousin (maternal) - (M) Wlid khaly / (F) bent khaly / (P)(M) wlaad khaly / (P)(F) bnaat khaly
I need	Khasny
Right now	Dooka
Night	Lil
To see	Tshoof
Light	Do
Outside	Barra
Without	Bla
Happy	Farhan
I see / I am seeing	Rani nchouf

I am saying no / I say no
Rani nqool la / qolt la
I want to see this today
Rani heb nshoof hada el-yom
I am with you everywhere
Rani ma'ak f kol plasse/partout
I am happy without my cousins here
Rani farhaan bla wlad 'ammy hna
I need to be there at night
Lazem nkoon temma f'lil
I see light outside
Rani nchouf do berra
What time is it right now?
Sh-hal sa'a douka?

* "My" / *dyali* is also a possessive pronoun. *Dyali* means "my" but also becomes a suffix to a noun. Referring to something of possession or related to me we use "y" For example:
-"cousin" / *wild el aam*, "my cousin" / *wild aam*
-"cup" / *kass*, "my cup" / *kassy*
For second and third person masculine noun, *wlid* ("son"), male (s.) *ak*, (p.) *kom*, and female (s.) *ik*, (p.) *kum*. "His" – *o* / "hers" – *ha*, noun endings will be *o* (for male) and *a* (for female). For example: "your son" / *wlidek* (m.), *wlidik* (f.), "your (plural) son" / *wlidkom*, "his son" / *wlido*, "her son" / *wlidha*, "our son" / *wlidna*, "their son" /*wlidhoum*
For second and third person feminine noun: "car" / *tumobil*. For example: "your car" / *tumobiltak*, "your (plural) car" / *tumobiltkom*, "his car" / *tumobilto*, "her car" /*tumobiltha*, "our car" / *tumobiltna*, "their car" / *tumobilthom*
*In Algerian Arabic "I want" is *habit*, however "I need" is *khasny*, in this program both will be used interchangeably. While *lazem* means "I must".
* This *isn't* a phrase book! The purpose of this book is *solely* to provide you with the tools to create *your own* sentences!

The Program

Place	Plassa
Easy	Sahla
To find	Telqa
To look for/to search	Thawess
Near / Close	Qrib
To wait	T'sana
To sell	Tbe'ee / (to be sold) – tenba'a
To use	N'sayé
To know	Ta'areff
To decide	T'khayer
Between	Mabeen / Been
Both	L'zouj
To	L'
Next to	Qdam

This place it's easy to find
Hada el-plassa sahla talqaha
I want to look for this next to the car
Habit nhawess aa'la hadi qdam el tomobil
I am saying to wait until tomorrow
Rani nqolek asana hatta el ghadwa
This table is easy to sell (to be sold)
Had tabla sahla lel be'ee (tenbaa')
I want to use this
Habit n'sayé hadi
I need to know where (location) is the house
Rani hab na'aref win jaya el dar
I want to decide between both places
Rani hab nkhayer mabin had zouj playesse

*Please pay close attention to the conjugation of verbs, whether they are in first person, second, or third. Unlike Anglo-Germanic languages, Latin languages, or even Classical Arabic, in which the first verb is conjugated and the following is always infinitive, in colloquial Arabic, it is quite different. The first verb is conjugated and the following one is conjugated as well. Keep in mind: The Algerian dialect of the Arabic language is considered a colloquial, rather than an official language.
*In Algerian Arabic, "to sell" is (M) *ybee'* / (F) *tbee'* For "to be sold," however, we use *lelbee'*.

Because	Aa'la jal/par ce-que
To buy	Tashreei
They, them	Hooma
Their	Tahoom
Beach	Shatt
Book	Ktab
Mine	Dyali
To understand	Tafham
Problem / Problems	Mushkel/(p)mashakil
I do / I am doing	Ndir / rani n'dir
Of	De
To look	Tshoof
Myself	Rouhi /Nafssi
Enough	Bazzaf
Food / water	Makla / ma
Each/ every/ entire/ all	Kool
Hotel	Otel / fondoq

I like this hotel because I want to look at the beach
Ana nheb had l-otel parceque nhab nshoof el-shatt
I want to buy a bottle of water
Rani hab nachri qar'aa maa
I do this every day
Ndir hadi kool yom
Both of them have enough food
L'zouj fihoum aa'andhoum bezzaf makla
That is the book, and that book is mine
Haw lik l'ktab, w hadak el ktab dyali
I need to understand the problem
Lazem nafham el moushkil
I see the view of the city from the hotel
Rani nchouf ga'aa la ville mel otel
I do my homework today
N'dir wadaeefi el manzyliya l'youm
My entire life (all my life)
Kooll hayaty/omri

*In Algerian Arabic, "problem" can either be *mushkel*, (plural) *mashakil*, or *problem*. The later which is derived from French.

The Program

I like	Nheb
There is / There are	Kayen
Family / Parents	Familya/aayla/waldiya
Why	Wa'alesh / 'Alash
To say	Tqool
Something	Haja
To go	Trouh
Ready	Wajed
Soon	Qrib
To work	Tkhdem
Who	Shkoon
To know	Ta'aref
That (conjunction)	Beli

I like to be at my house with my parents
Nheb nkoon f'dari ma'a waldiya
I want to know why I need to say something important
Ani hab na'aref aa'lash lazem nqool haja mohyma
I am there with him
Rani hna ma'ah
I am busy, but I need to be ready soon
Rani mashghool, bassah lazem nkoon wajed qrib
I like to go to work
Nheb nrooh nakhdem
Who is there?
Shkoon hna?
I want to know if they are here, because I want to go outside
Habit na'aref ila rahoom hna, parceque habit nrouh barra
There are seven dolls
Kayen sab'aa popyette
I need to know that that's a good idea
Habit na'aref beli hadi bonne idée/ fikra mliha

*In the last sentence, we use "that" as a conjunction (*beli*) and a demonstrative pronoun *hadi*.
*In Algerian Arabic, "to work" is *tkhdem*. Masculine form is *yekhdem* and feminine form is *takhdem*.

How much /How many	Sh-hal
To bring	Tjeeb
With me	Ma'aya
Instead	Fi ood
Only	Ghir/ Bark
When	Waqtah / Ki
I can / Can I	Naqder / ila naqder
Or	Wala
Were	Kanoo
Without me	Bala beya
Fast	Bel khef
Slow	Bela'aqel
Cold	Bard
Inside	L'dakhel
To eat	Takool
Hot	Skhoon
To Drive	Tsoog

How much money do I need to bring with me?
Sesh-haal drahem yelzemli njeeb m'aaya?
Instead of this cake, I want that cake
Fi ood had el gato, Habit had el gato
Only when you can
Ghir ki taqder
They were without me yesterday
Hooma kanoo Bala beeya elbareh
Do I need to drive the car fast or slow?
Est-ce que lazemli nsoog tomobil belkhef wela bla'aqel?
It is cold inside the library
Kayen el bard dakhel el-maktabah
Yes, I like to eat this hot for my lunch
Ih, nheb nakool hady skhoona fel el ftoor
I can work today
Naqder nekdhem el-yom

*"Were" is *kanoo*, but for "they were," "We were" is *konna*.
*In Algerian Arabic *est ce que* is used to represent "do."

The Program

To answer	Njaweb/t'répondi
To fly	Teer
Time / Times	Marra / Mrrat
To travel	T'voyagé / Tsafer
To learn	Tet'allam/(M) yt'alam/(F)tet'alam
How	Keefash
To swim	T'oom/(M)y'oom/(F) to'oom
To practice	T'sayi
To play	Tel'eb
To leave	Tkheli/t'abondonné
Many /much /a lot	Bezaaf
I go to	Nrouh l'
First	Lawel
World	Aalem

I want to answer many questions
Ani heb njaweb bezzaf as-eela
I must fly to Dubai today
Lazem nteer l'Dubai lyom
I need to learn how to swim at the pool
Lazem nt'aalem kifech no'oom f la piscine
I want to learn to play better tennis
Ani heb nt'aalem nala'ab mlih tennis
I want to leave this here for you when I go to travel the world
Ani heb nkheli hadi hna lik ki nrouh n'voyagé el aalem
Since the first time
Men l'marra lawla
The children are yours
Drari dyawlek?

*In Algerian Darja Arabic, "to leave (school)" is *thabess*. "To leave (a place)" is *trouh*.

*In Algerian Arabic, there are three definitions for time:
-"time" / *mudda* refers to "era", "moment period," "duration of time."
-"time(s)" / *marra(t)* / *karra(t)* refers to "occasion" or "frequency."
-"time" / *sa'a* references "hour," "what time is it?"

*In Algerian Arabic, "to answer", as in "answer the phone," is *t'répondi*; to answer a question is *jaweb*.

*With the knowledge you've gained so far, now try to create your own sentences!

Conversational Arabic Quick and Easy

Nobody / Anyone	Hatta wahed/n'importe qui
Against	Did do / Contre
Us	Hna
To visit	T'visité
Mom / Mother	Yemma / yemmat
To give	Ta'aty
Which	Shkoon
To meet	Tetlaqa
Someone	Kech wahad
Just	Gheir
To walk	Tamshy
Around	Au tour
Towards	Jihet
Than	Min
Nothing	Waloo / hata haja

Something is better than nothing
Haja khir min waloo
I am against him
Ana did'do / contro
Is there anyone here?
Kayen kech wahed hna?
We go to visit my family each week
Nrouh n'visité familya ta'ee kool smana
I need to give you something
Lazemli n'mdlek haja
Do you want to go meet someone?
Est-ce que rak heb trouh tetlaqa kech wahed?
I was here on Wednesdays as well
Ana kont hna chaque arba' tani
Do you do this every day?
Est-ce que dir hadi kool yom?
You need to walk around, but not towards the house
Lazemlek tetdrab dora bassah mashi jihet el dar

*In Arabic, when using the pronoun "you" as a direct and indirect object pronoun (the person who is actually affected by the action that is being carried out) in relation to a verb, the pronoun "you" becomes a suffix to that verb. That suffix becomes *ak* (masc.) *ik* (fem.).
- "to give" / *ta'aty*: "to give you" / *na'tylek*
- "to tell" / *tqool*: "to tell you" / *yqoolak* (m.), *tqoolak* (f.)
- "see you" / *nshoofak*: "to see you" (plural) / *nshoofkom*
For third person male, add *o* and *on* for plural, for female add *a* and *on* for plural.
- "tell him" / *qoolo*
- "tell her" / *qoolelha*
- "see them" / *shoofhom*
- "see us "/ *shoofna*

The Program

I have	'Andy
Don't	Mashy
Friend	Saheb
To borrow	Tslef
To look like / resemble	Ychabah
Grandfather	Jedd
To want	Theb
To stay	Trayah
To continue	Tkamel
Way	Triq
I don't	Ana mashy
To show	Twary
To prepare	Twajed
I am not going	Ma rani rayeh
Like (preposition)	Shbah
Algiers	Alger/l'dzayer

Do you want to look like Salim
Est-ce que habit tchbah l'Salim
I want to borrow this book for my grandfather
Habit n'ssalef hed el kteb l'jeddy
I want to drive and to continue on this way to my house
Habit n'ssog wa nkamel f had el trig l'dary
I have a friend there, that's why I want to stay in Algiers
'Andy sahby temma, alabiha habit nrayah fi Alger.
I am not going to see anyone here
Ma rani rayeh nshoof hatta wahed hna
I need to show you how to prepare breakfast
Lazem nwarilek kifesh twajed ftor sbah
Why don't you have the book?
'Alash ma'andekshe l-ktab?
That is incorrect, I don't need the car today
Hada mashy sah, ana ma khasnishe l-twmwbil l-yom

To remember	Tetfaker
Your, yours	Ta'ak
Number	Numéro (French) / raqm
Hour	Sa'aa
Dark / darkness	Dalma
About / on the	'Ala
Grandmother	Man
Five	Khamsa
Minute / Minutes	Dqeeqa
More	Zeed
To think	Tkhamem
To do	Deer
To come	Tji
To hear	Tsma'
Last	Lakher

You need to remember my number
Lazem tetfaker numéro dyalli
This is the last hour of darkness
Hady akher Sa'aa ta'a dalma
I want to come and to hear my grandmother speak Arabic
Rani heb nji w nssma'a many tahder arbiya
I need to think more about this, and what to do
Lzemli nkhamem kter aa'la hadi w wesh lazem ndir
From here to there, it's only five minutes
Min hena lel hih, khams dqayq bark
The school on the mountain
L'madrassa fel l'jabal

*In Algerian Arabic "school" can either be *madrassa* or *msid*.

The Program

To leave	Tkhroj
Again	T'aawed
Algeria	Dzayer / L'Algeery
To take	Takhod
To try	T'ssayé
To rent	Tekry
Without her	Bala beeha
We are	Hna
To turn off	Tafi
To ask	Tssaqssy
To stop	T'habess
Permission	Ydn / Autorisation
Building	Batima
To sleep	Narqood
He needs	Hwa khaso

He needs to leave and rent a house at the beach
Lazem yakhrouj w yakri dar aa'la l'bhar
I want to take the test without her
Habit ndir el- test bla beeha
We are here a long time
Rana hna waqt kbir
I need to turn off the lights early tonight
Lzemli ntafi do bakri hed lila
We want to stop here
Habina nhabssoo dooka
We are from Annaba
Hna men Annaba
The same building
Nafss el batima
I want to ask permission to leave
Habit n'demandé el ydn nakhroudj
I want to sleep
Habit narqood

*In Algerian Darja Arabic, "to stop" is *thabess*, "to cease" is also *waqf*.

*In Algerian Arabic, "permission" can either be *ydn, autorisation* or *permission*. The last two are derived from French.

To open	Taftah
A bit, a little, a little bit	Shweeya
To pay	Tkhaless
Once again	Tany
There isn't/ there aren't	Mafi
Sister	Okht
To hope	Tetmana
To live	T'eesh
Nice to meet you	Metsharfeen
Name	Ism
Last name	Laqeb
To return	Twelly
Morocco	Maroc / al-maghreb
Door	Bab

I need to open the door for my sister
Lzemli nftah elbaab l-khty
I need to buy something
Lazemli nshry haja
I want to meet your sisters
Lzemli natlaqa Khiyatek
Nice to meet you, what is your name and your last name
Metsharfin, weshnou howa asmek w laqbek?
To hope for a little better
Tetmana shwya khyr
I want to return from the United States and to live in Qatar without problems
Habit nwelli men marikan w n'eesh fi Qatar bla mashakeel
Why are you sad right now?
Wa'alesh rak hzin douka?
There aren't any people here
Makan hetta wahed hna
There isn't enough time to go to Blida today
Makech bezzafel - waqt bech nrouh l'Blida l'yoma

*This *isn't* a phrase book! The purpose of this book is *solely* to provide you with the tools to create *your own* sentences!

The Program

To happen	Ykoon / yassra
To order	T'cmandé
To drink	Tachrab
Excuse me	(M) Smah ly/(F) samhy ly
Child	(M) Tfel, (F) Tafla
Woman	Mra
To begin / To start	Tebda
To finish	Tkamel
To help	T'aawen
To smoke	Tetkayef
To love	Theb
To talk / To Speak	Tahder

This must happen today
Hada Lazem ykoon l-yom
Excuse me, my child is here as well
Smah le, wlidi hna tani
I love you
Nhabek
I see you
Rani nshoofek
I need you at my side
Nssahqek fi djenby
I need to begin soon to be able to finish at 3 o'clock in the afternoon
Lazemli nadba bekri bech/mesh nakel a'ala 3 ta'a l'aashia.
I need help
Lzemli ma'awna
I don't want to smoke once again
Maranish heb ntkayef tani
I want to learn how to speak Arabic
Habit nta'alem nahder arbiya.

To read	Teqra
To write	Tekteb
To teach	Teta'alem
To close	T'ghleq
To choose	T'khayer
To prefer	T'heb /t'fadel
To put	T'hatt
Less	Qal
Sun	Shamss
Month	Sh'ar
I Talk	Tahder
Exact	Sah / exact

I need this book to learn how to read and write in Arabic because I want to teach in Egypt
Ana khasny had l-ktab nt'aalem keefash nqra w nktob bel 'arabiya parceque habit neqeri fi masr

I want to close the door of the house
Habit naghleq bab el dar

I prefer to put the gift here
Habit nhatt had el cado hna

I want to pay less than you for the dinner
Habit nkhless chouiya alik lel aa'cha

I speak with the boy and the girl in French
Nahder ma'a tfel w tefla bel francais

There is sun outside today
Kayen shamss barra l-yom

Is it possible to know the exact date?
Moomkeen n'aref la date exact?

*With the knowledge you've gained so far, now try to create your own sentences!

The Program

To exchange (*money*)	Tbadel
To call	T'aayet
Brother	Akh
Dad	'Ab
To sit	Tqo'od
Together	Kif kif
To change	Tbadel
Of course	Sah
Welcome	Marahba
During	Fel
Years	(S)'Aam/ (P) 'a'awam
Sky	Sma
Up	Foq
Down	Taht
Sorry	Smahli
To follow	Tbaa'
To the	L'
Big	Kbir
New	Jdid
Never / ever	Jamais / à jamais
Him / her	O / a (*read footnote*)

I don't want to exchange this money at the bank
Mahabitsh nbadel had drahem fel-banka

I want to call my brother and my dad today
Habeet na'ayet l'khooya wel baba el 'yom

Of course I can come to the theater, and I want to sit together with you and with your sister
Tah sah nqder nji l'cineema, w habit nqa'adoo kif kif ma'ak w khtek

I need to go down to see your new house
Lazemli nji ma'ak nshoof darek el djdida

I can see the sky from the window
naqder nshoof e-sama min el taqa

I am sorry, but he wants to follow her to the store
Samhli, bsah hab ytaba'aha lel-hanoot

I don't ever want to see you again
Manishe hab nzid nshoofek tan

*In Algerian Darja dialect, brother is *akh*, and dad is *ab*. However, "my dad" is *baba* and "my brother" is *khoya*. "My sister" is *khty*, and "my mother" is *yemma*.
*For the possessive pronouns, her (*ha*) and him (*o*), both become suffixes to the verb or noun. Concerning nouns: her house / *darha*, his house / *daro*. Concerning cases regarding verbs, please see footnotes on page #19.

To allow	Tsmah
To believe	Tamen
Morning	Sbah
Except	Ma 'ada
To promise	T'promé
Good night	Layla sa'eeda
Street	Trig
People	Naas
To move	T'bougé
Far	B'eed
Different	Mbdel
Man	Rajil
To enter	Tetdkhel
To receive	T'recevé
Throughout	Men
Good afternoon	Masa elkheir
Left / right	Gauche / droite
Nice/pleasant	Mlah

I need to allow him to go with us, he is a different man now
Lazemli nkhelih yji ma'anna, rahou rajel wahed okher douka
I believe everything except this
Na'amen koolshy ma 'ada hady
I promise to say good night to my parents each night
Nawa'ad nqool bonne nuit l'waldiya koul lila.
The people from Jordan are very pleasant
Nass el ordon bezaaf mlah
I need to find another hotel very quickly
Lazemli nelqa otel akher rapidement
They need to receive a book for work
Lazemlhoom y'receveiw ktab lel khadma
I see the sun in the morning
Rani nshoof shamss f'sbah
The house is on the right side of the street
El dar rahy fel coté droit/ jiha el yomna ta'a trig

*In Algerian Arabic, "good night" can either be *layla sa'eeda* or *bonne nuit*. The later which is derived from French.

The Program

To wish	Tmanna
Bad	A'ayane/mashy mliha
To Get	Takhod
To forget	Tenssa
Everybody / Everyone	Koll shakhss
Although	Malgré que (French)
To feel	Thass
Great	Mohim
Next (as in close, near)	Qdem
To like	Theb
In front	En face
Person	Shakhs
Behind	Mor
Well	Mleeh
Goodbye	Bess lama
Restaurant	Restorant
Bathroom	Beit el maa / twalet
Next (as in next year)	Jay

I don't want to wish you anything bad
Maranish hab ntmanalek haja mashy mliha
I must forget everybody from my past to feel well
Lazem nenssa ga'a nass ta'a l'passé bech nhess rouhi mleeh
I am next to the person behind you
Rani qdem el sharss li morak
There is a great person in front of me
Kayen shakhs mohim qaddami
I say goodbye to my friends
Qolt Bess lama l's'haby
Where is the bathroom in the restaurant?
Win les twalet fel restorant?
She has to get a car before the next year
Lazem tjib tomobil qbel el'aam jay
I like the house, but it is very small
Nhab el dar, bssah bezzaf sghira

To remove / to take out	Tnahee
Please	Men fadlek
Beautiful	(M)Chbab, (F) Chaba
To lift	Terfed
Include / Including	Yadkhoul fih/Yashmol
Belong	Ta'a
To hold	Tshedd
To check	T'vérifié
Small	Sgheer
Real	Haqeeqy
Week	Smana
Size	Taille
Even though	Meme si / malgré
Doesn't	Mashy
So (as in "then")	Ya'ny
So (as in "very")	Bezaaf
Price	Souma / pri

She wants to remove this door please
Hiya habet tnahi hed el bab men fadlek
This doesn't belong here, I need to check again
Hady mashy ta'a hna, lzemli n'vériyé tani
This week the weather was very beautiful
Had el smana el hal kan chbab bezaaf
I need to know which is the real diamond
Lazemli na'aref wesh howa diamond ta'a sah
We need to check the size of the house
Lazemna n'vérifiyiw la taille ta'a dar
I want to lift this, so you need to hold it high
Habit nerfed hady, alors lazemlek tefadha a'aliya
I can pay this even though that the price is expensive
Naqder nkhaless malgré souma ghalya
Including everything, is this price correct?
Dakhel koolesh, had l'souma shiha?

*In Algerian Arabic, "please" can either be *men fadlek* or *s'il vous plait*. The later which is derived from French.

Countries of the Middle East
Baldan el-sharq' el- awsatt

Lebanon	Loobnan
Syria	Sourya
Jordan	L-ordon
Israel/Palestine/West Bank	Isra'eel/Falasteen/al-dyffa algharbiyya
Iraq	L'iraq
Saudi Arabia	Al-so'odya
Kuwait	L'kwait
Qatar	Gatar
Bahrain	L-bahrein
United Arab Emirates	L'emarat al'arabya el-motaheda
Oman	'Oman
Yemen	L-yaman
Egypt	Masr
Libya	Leebya
Tunisia	Toones
Algeria	Dzayer / L'Algeery
Morocco	Marok / al-maghreb

Months

January	Janvier
February	Fevrier
March	Mars
April	Avril
May	May
June	Juin
July	Juillet
August	Aout
September	Septembre
October	Octobre
November	Novembre
December	Décembre

Days of the Week

Sunday	Al-ahad
Monday	Al-tanein
Tuesday	Al-tlatha'
Wednesday	L-arba'
Thursday	Al-khmees
Friday	Jam'aa
Saturday	Sabt

Seasons

Spring	Rbee'
Summer	Seif
Autumn	Khreef
Winter	Shtta

Cardinal Directions

North	Shamaal/Nord
South	Janoob / sud
East	Sharq / Est
West	Gharb / West

Colors

Black	Khal
White	Byad
Gray	Gri
Red	Hmar
Blue	Zreq
Yellow	Sfar
Green	Khdar
Orange	Orange
Purple	Violé
Brown	Marron

Numbers

One	Wahed
Two	Zuj
Three	Tlatah
Four	Rab'aa
Five	Khamsa
Six	Satta
Seven	Sab'aa
Eight	Tmenya
Nine	Tasa'a
Ten	'Ashra

Twenty	'Eshreen
Thirty	Tlaten
Forty	Arb'aaeen
Fifty	Khamseen
Sixty	Sitteen
Seventy	Saba'aeen
Eighty	Tmaneen
Ninety	Tisi'in
Hundred	Myya
Thousand	Alf / Mille
Million	Mellyoon

CONCLUSION

Congratulations! You have completed all the tools needed to master the Arabic language, and I hope that this has been a valuable learning experience. Now you have sufficient communication skills to be confident enough to embark on a visit to an Arab speaking country in North Africa, impress your friends, and boost your resume so good luck.

This program is available in other languages as well, and it is my fervent hope that my language learning programs will be used for good, enabling people from all corners of the globe and from all cultures and religions to be able to communicate harmoniously. After memorizing the required three hundred and fifty words, please perform a daily five-minute exercise by creating sentences in your head using these words. This simple exercise will help you grasp conversational communications even more effectively. Also, once you memorize the vocabulary on each page, follow it by using a notecard to cover the words you have just memorized and test yourself and follow that by going back and using this same notecard technique on the pages you studied during the previous days. This repetition technique will assist you in mastering these words in order to provide you with the tools to create your own sentences.

Every day, use this notecard technique on the words that you have just studied.

Everything in life has a catch. The catch here is just consistency. If you just open the book, and after the first few pages of studying the program, you put it down, then you will not gain anything. However, if you consistently dedicate a half hour daily to studying, as well as reviewing what you have learned from previous days, then you will quickly realize why this method is the most effective technique ever created to become conversational in a foreign language. My technique works! For anyone who doubts this technique, all I can say is that it has worked for me and hundreds of others.

Note from the Author

Thank you for your interest in my work. I encourage you to share your overall experience of this book by posting a review. Your review can make a difference! Please feel free to describe how you benefited from my method or provide creative feedback on how I can improve this program. I am constantly seeking ways to enhance the quality of this product, based on personal testimonials and suggestions from individuals like you.

Thanks and best of luck,
Yatir Nitzany

www.ingramcontent.com/pod-product-compliance
Lightning Source LLC
Chambersburg PA
CBHW052056110526
44591CB00013B/2240